By Larry McMurtry

When the Light Goes
Telegraph Days
Oh What a Slaughter
The Colonel and Little Missie
Loop Group
Folly and Glory
By Sorrow's River
The Wandering Hill
Sin Killer
Sacagawea's Nickname: Essays on the American West
Paradise
Boone's Lick
Roads
Still Wild: A Collection of Western Stories
Walter Benjamin at the Dairy Queen
Duane's Depressed
Crazy Horse
Comanche Moon
Dead Man's Walk
The Late Child
Streets of Laredo
The Evening Star
Buffalo Girls
Some Can Whistle
Anything for Billy
Film Flam: Essays on Hollywood
Texasville
Lonesome Dove
The Desert Rose
Cadillac Jack
Somebody's Darling
Terms of Endearment
All My Friends Are Going to Be Strangers
Moving On
The Last Picture Show
In a Narrow Grave: Essays on Texas
Leaving Cheyenne
Horseman, Pass By

By Larry McMurtry and Diana Ossana

Pretty Boy Floyd
Zeke and Ned

BOOKS:

A MEMOIR

Larry McMurtry

SIMON & SCHUSTER

New York • London • Toronto • Sydney

SIMON & SCHUSTER
1230 Avenue of the Americas
New York, NY 10020

First Simon & Schuster hardcover edition July 2008

SIMON & SCHUSTER and colophon are registered trademarks
of Simon & Schuster, Inc.

For information about special discounts for bulk purchases,
please contact Simon & Schuster Special Sales at
1-800-456-6798 or business@simonandschuster.com

Designed by Dana Sloan

Manufactured in the United States of America

10 9 8 7 6 5 4 3 2 1

Library of Congress Cataloging-in-Publication Data

McMurtry, Larry.
    Books : a memoir / Larry McMurtry.—1st Simon & Schuster hardcover ed.
        p.   cm.
    1. McMurtry, Larry—Books and reading. 2. McMurtry, Larry—Child-
hood and youth. 3. Antiquarian booksellers—United States—Biography.
4. Novelists, American—20th century—Biography. 5. McMurtry, Larry—
Homes and haunts—Texas. I. Title.
    PS3563.A319Z46 2008
    813'.54—dc22
ISBN 13: 978-1-4165-8334-9
ISBN 10:   1-4165-8334-3

For the faithful

Marcia Carter
William F. Hale and Candee Harris
Khristal Collins
and
Julie and Cody Ressell of Three Dog Books,
without whose efforts there would be no Booked Up

And from the Bookstop in Tucson, Arizona

Claire
Tina
Kate
Rachel (emerita)

May they ever flourish.

BOOKS: A MEMOIR

I

I don't remember either of my parents ever reading me a story—perhaps that's why I've made up so many. They were good parents, but just not story readers. In 1936, when I was born, the Depression sat heavily on all but the most fortunate, a group that didn't include us. My McMurtry grandparents were both still alive, and my mother and father and I lived in their house, which made for frequent difficulties. Sometimes there was a cook and a resident cowboy—where they bunked, I'm not sure. The fifty yards or so between the house and the barn boiled with poultry. My first enemies were hens, roosters, peacocks, turkeys. We ate lots of the hens, but our consumption of turkeys, peacocks, and roosters was, to my young mind, inexcusably slow.

I believe my grandfather, William Jefferson McMurtry, who died when I was four, *did* tell me stories, but they were all stories about his adventures as a Texas pioneer and, so far as I can remember, did not include imaginary beings, such as one might find in Grimm or Andersen.

My grandfather told me these stories about himself while sitting on the roof of the storm cellar, a dank cell to which we often repaired at inconvenient times—both my mother and my grandmother were paranoid about tornadoes. Any dark cloud might send us scuttling downward, into a place that, as I discovered early, was not scorpion free.

Our ranch house, which my father and my grandfather built from plans purchased from Montgomery Ward—usually the supplier was just

1

called Monkey Ward—was a simple shotgun house, three bedrooms and a bath on the south side, simple hall, kitchen, dining room, living room on the north side. We rarely used the living room, although my grandfather was laid out in it, once he died. It did have a fireplace, into which my grandfather, before his death, often spat copiously.

As a very small child I was awed by the amount of spit he could summon—I didn't realize that most of it was tobacco juice.

Of books there were none. Some of my older cousins tell me that my grandmother, Louisa Francis McMurtry, was a woman with lots of curiosity, who once subscribed to all the magazines. Where did they go? The only magazine I can remember seeing in the ranch house was *The Cattleman,* the trade journal of the range cattle industry, which once ran an article on our family called "McMurtry Means Beef." Since the nine McMurtry boys were all cattlemen on varying scales, that seemed to be fair enough, even though a couple of the brothers came perilously close to being farmers: quite a different gestalt, of course. Of the three sisters only the eldest, Grace, married into agriculture. I remember visiting Aunt Grace once, and the place we visited, in the Texas panhandle, seemed to me to be a farm. But possibly it too was really a ranch.

Nothing was more evident about my father than that he hated farming, he himself being a cattleman, pure and simple, amen.

Still, it puzzles me how totally bookless our ranch house was. There must have been a Bible, but I don't remember ever seeing it. My father did read the range cattle books of J. Frank Dobie, but the only one I remember seeing in our house, which, by this time, was a small house in the village of Archer City, was *The Longhorns,* which I borrowed for my father from Mr. Will Taylor, a wealthy and elderly oilman who lived in a great mansion just south of our hay field.

I now own Mr. Taylor's mansion and have filled it with about twenty-eight thousand books, which took a while.

My father's reason for needing a book to read in the daytime, when he would normally have been working, was that, inconveniently, he had caught mumps in his fiftieth year: thus was idleness forced upon him.

The fact of the bookless ranch house meant that before the age of five or six I lived in an aural culture. My mother, father, grandfather, grandmother, and whatever uncles or cowboys happened by, sat on the front porch every night in good weather and told stories; but they were seldom stories that held much interest for a young child. What did I care that Uncle Charlie, the oldest son, had defied his parents and been beaten with an ironweed switch, ironweed being a sturdy weed that did not fray quickly when a rebel was being switched. What Uncle Charlie did to earn this punishment I never found out, but his brothers agreed that he remained defiant, ironweed or no.

Uncle Charlie, in the fifties, would occasionally host a family reunion, always at a country club just outside the bleak panhandle town of Clarendon. Those were the only times I saw him, and I cannot remember him uttering a sound. I believe he had had some trouble with wives—enough that he had learned to hold his tongue.

2

THE CASUAL, STORYTELLING culture of my early childhood was soon augmented by a powerful new force: radio. When I was four, World War II broke out, transforming millions of lives, including the lives of the little group that gathered nightly on the porch of our ranch house. My grandfather McMurtry had died. But the rest of us, which meant a shifting population of visitors, cowboys, indigents, cousins, and the like, listened faithfully to the war news, every night.

My father, then in his forties, was too old for service, but once America entered the war, nearly everyone knew someone local who was now overseas. Our concern was high.

At the age of five or six, war news didn't grip me much, though I was happy to be a junior plane spotter, and would often climb the windmill, expecting to see enemy aircraft swooping over the mesquite pastures and sorghum fields of home.

At the time, my aunt Naomi, one of my mother's sisters, lived nearby with her husband, J. K. Mitchell, who was foreman of an adjacent ranch. I saw her often, along with my cousins J.K. and Mary Louise. One day, at our ranch house, my aunt casually mentioned Flopsy, Mopsy, and Cottontail, characters she seemed to assume I would be familiar with. But I *wasn't* familiar with them. So far as I can now recall, they were the first imagined characters I had ever been told about.

But what exactly were they? They sounded like rabbits, in which our ranch abounded; but it abounded in long-legged, long-eared jackrabbits, none of whom fit the names Flopsy, Mopsy, and Cottontail.

I was very puzzled by this, because I didn't realize, at the time, that there could be made-up stories. At that point I was accustomed to concerning myself with things that clearly existed, particularly poultry, a constant threat to one as small as I was. Reality, such as it was on our ranch, required unwavering vigilance if one were not to be pecked by the poultry, kicked by a mule, or the like.

This was the age at which I might have been expected to make up an imaginary friend, but, a realist from the git-go, I failed to do this. Real things that were bad things often happened: once my father nearly cut his arm off in the thresher. I can still see him walking up from the field with one side of his shirt drenched in blood—of which he lost a lot. But he survived, and kept his arm.

Then my dog Scraps got bitten by a rattlesnake and died. This was long before the organized snake hunts, when rattlers were plentiful—with a consequent reduction of the rodent population and, unfortunately, of the small-dog population too.

Of course, far away, World War II was happening—but I did not really know what war was. At night, on the porch, while the adults tried to absorb the news of distant battles, I mainly watched the cars and trucks moving up and down Highway 281, a major Canada-to-Mexico artery. I wondered where those cars and trucks were going, day after day and night after night, endlessly, relentlessly. Many years later I answered that question and described where the road went in a book called *Roads*.

With the day-to-day life of our ranch being so crowded, I somehow failed to get around to fantasy—to story, to invention—until one day in 1942 when my cousin Robert Hilburn, on his way to enlist in the new war, stopped by the ranch house and gave me the gift that changed my life.

The gift was a box containing nineteen books.

3

To MY REGRET I never got to know Robert Hilburn well. On his return from the Pacific Theater he stopped by our house again—by then we were living in Archer City—and gave me a Japanese rifle. Though an ugly thing, it was, for a time, my most prized possession, and I still have it.

I had, by this time, read the nineteen books he had given me to tatters. They were standard boys' adventure books of the thirties, on the order of *Jerry Todd in the Whispering Cave* or *Poppy Ott and the Stuttering Parrot*. The first book I actually read was an adventure involving the Canadian Mounties, called *Sergeant Silk: The Prairie Scout*. Some years later, while browsing in the Bookstop, in Tucson (a wonderful shop), I spotted a copy of *Sergeant Silk* and bought it, the copy in the original box having long since been lost.

I recall that I was sick in bed the day Robert Hilburn brought in the box of books. In my sixth and seventh years I was often in bed, closeted like a tiny Proust, while I listened to the radio from sign-on until sign-off. The necessity of taking an eighty-mile school-bus ride, in the company of older farm children whose behavior verged on the brutish, was too much for me. My parents and teachers recognized this—they let me cut the second semester of the first grade, during which we moved to Archer City, to facilitate the education of myself and the three siblings who were to follow: Sue, Judy, Charlie.

I remember that I started reading *Sergeant Silk: The Prairie Scout*—a random choice—the minute Robert Hilburn left my room. What I don't remember is how I learned to read. In early 1942 I had only briefly been to school, and no one, that I can recall, bothered about teaching me my ABC's.

Yet I *could* read, and reading very quickly came to seem what I was meant to do. It was a decade or more before I came to hope that books would somehow provide me with a vocation, as they have. For a long time I didn't know what kind of vocation one could make of reading, which, after all, is still the core activity where books are concerned. I didn't, at first, aspire to write books, and I was in my mid-twenties before I began to hope that maybe I could become an antiquarian book seller, which I have now been for about fifty years.

At first, when I began to trade in books a little, book selling was mainly a way to finance my reading: sell a book you don't want to read and, with the money, buy a book you do want to read. I no longer need book selling to finance my reading, and yet, if worse came to worst, it would. More than three hundred thousand books are available for sale in Archer City, in the stock of Booked Up and Three Dog Books, our neighbors and friends.

It may be that the presence of all this knowledge is mostly an irritant to the locals, but there's not much they can do about it—but this is to jump some ways ahead. There have been many stages to my life as a reader-writer-bookman, and I'd like to return for a bit to the earlier stages, when my personal library—now some twenty-eight thousand volumes strong—consisted precisely of nineteen books. Forming that library, and reading it, is surely one of the principal achievements of my life.

4
_____

BIOLOGY MAY BE destiny, as a famous thinker claimed; but then, I would contend, geography is destiny too. I was born in a part of Texas that is essentially Midwestern. Small towns in my part of Texas don't differ that much from towns in Kansas or Nebraska. These are towns where change comes slowly—and yet it comes.

I think it was important for the development of my reading that Robert Hilburn gave me the nineteen books while we still lived in the country—isolated, that is, from town life. I read all those books at once, and reread most of them several times. There was radio, of course, and radio was quite important in my life; but radio was aural. Where reading was concerned, the nineteen books still had a monopoly on my attention. I knew there must be other books, probably better books, somewhere, but until we moved to town I had no way to get to them.

It was only after our move to Archer City—a move my father accepted with reluctance—that we entered the middle class. On the ranch we had been more or less classless country people. The mere possession of a house in town—though it was a small, ugly house, of no distinction—changed things. First, we got a subscription to *Reader's Digest*, which soon included a chance to buy Reader's Digest Condensed Books, which I hated on sight and still hate. I always wanted the whole story or nothing.

At about the same time my mother subscribed to *Good Housekeeping* and *Ladies' Home Journal,* indispensable sources of domestic information for the middle-class housewife of the day.

Fast on the heels of *Reader's Digest* came the door-to-door encyclopedia salesman, who convinced my parents (more probably my mother) that we children would be sluggards, left far behind our contemporaries, if they failed to provide us with the *World Book Encyclopedia.* They bit and we got the *World Book.* Much later, as a bookman, I have been forced to reject hundreds if not thousands of sets of the *World Book,* which is as dead today as the dodo.

Along with the *World Book* we acquired the multivolumed children's anthology called *My Book House,* which gathered stories and folklore from world literature and reproduced them in simplified form, with many illustrations. I suspect *My Book House* was meant for the edification of my younger siblings—nonetheless, I read it several times, thereby making the acquaintance of Robin Hood, the Greek gods, Yggdrasil the immortal tree, and, maybe, Don Quixote.

I am a little bit uncertain about the last mentioned, Don Quixote, the character whose companion was Sancho Panza. I think I have speculated somewhere that *Don Quixote* was in the box of nineteen books, and that I read it sitting in the barn loft, or on the deck of the windmill, or somewhere at the ranch.

I now doubt these romantic memories. I don't think it *was* in the initial box. And yet I did read, early on, some simplified version of *Don Quixote,* which I could tell, even then, was a different order of book than *Poppy Ott and the Stuttering Parrot.* Possibly I got a copy from the school library, or it might have come as a present from one of my more literate aunts: Aunt Margaret, on my father's side, or Aunt Minta, on my mother's.

I can't be sure what abridgment I read, but I did realize that the crazy old knight and the peasant pragmatist were an essential pair, the ultimate source of Gus and Call, in *Lonesome Dove.* I eventually read all of *Don Quixote* in the Putnam translation, and have sampled two or three more recent translations, but, usually now, I read the first chapters and skip to the end, which I still find very moving, after many readings and in several translations.

What is important is that, early on, I read some version of *Don Quixote* and pondered the grave differences (comically cast) between Sancho and the Don. Between the two is where fiction, as I've mostly read and written it, lives.

5

AMONG THE VARIOUS legends that have accumulated around Thomas Pynchon is that while writing *V*—in my opinion a masterpiece—he read only the *N* volume of the *Encyclopaedia Britannica*. Well, there is the famous nose job, for which the *N* volume might have contributed a little, but I don't think I believe that story.

While teaching at Rice, in Houston, in the mid-sixties, I may have missed my chance to meet Thomas Pynchon—how was I to know he was going to disappear? He was said to be living somewhere near the Ship Channel; he was said to need work. I think I sent him a note saying I could probably find him a little teaching, and I think he sent me a polite note declining to become involved with academia, but I'm not sure either note was ever written. All I remember for sure now is that someone mentioned the part about the *N* volume to me.

At any rate, though I didn't at first realize the class significance of our owning a set of the *World Book Encyclopedia,* I became, for a time, an encyclopedia reader myself. Flipping through the volumes sometimes turned up interesting stuff: Genghis Khan, for example, sweeping down on Europe with his Mongol Horde.

There is education to be had from even a middle-class, middlebrow encyclopedia; for that matter probably all encyclopedias, including the *Britannica,* are done by and for the middle class. The exception would be the great French one done by Diderot and his team, which was done royally, before the middle class had risen to the position it holds today.

Certainly it was from the *World Book* that I had my first access to historical events. When, as a freshman at Rice, I took world history from the formidable Katherine Drew, I was able to keep a handhold on the slopes of history only because of things I had read for myself, in the *World Book*.

6

I HAVE MENTIONED, but not explained, why my having those nineteen books while we were still in the country was important to me. The reason is that, in our country isolation, I came to reading before I came to American popular culture generally—a culture represented, say, by comic books, movies, and (soon) paperbacks.

Our ranch house was about eighteen miles from Archer City. When I was a young child we went there seldom, usually making the whole journey on dirt roads. It was not until the fifties that a farm-to-market road made the trip easier.

Before we moved to Archer City I was taken there maybe twice a month, almost always on Saturday, when I could be parked for a couple of hours to see the traditional Saturday afternoon double feature, usually Westerns, one of which would probably star either Roy Rogers or Gene Autry.

During this interval my parents did their shopping.

This was the heyday of the Republic Pictures serials, many of them involving jungle queens or damsels otherwise in distress. From the first I liked the serials better than the feature films.* Columbia also made a

---

*Decades later, scholarly justice was finally done to the serials of Republic Pictures, in a folio-sized study called *Valley of the Cliffhangers*, by Jack Mathis, published in Northbrook, Illinois. In the stills from a serial called *Fighting Devil Dogs* the viewer will find an evil figure who looks just like Darth Vader.

There may by now be a companion volume on the serials of Columbia, but I haven't seen it.

lot of serials. As a young screenwriter I worked at Columbia, but not at Republic, whose film library was eventually purchased by Ted Turner. In Republic's last days I believe Dina Merrill co-owned it.

Had I been free to wander around the courthouse square, I imagine I would soon have wandered into the drugstore and discovered comic books. I *did* finally discover them, but at first I didn't like them very much. Neither Superman nor Batman interested me in the least. I wanted stronger stuff, and stronger stuff did soon arrive in the form of the many violent propaganda comics published by the Fiction House group: *Fight, Rangers, Wings,* even *Sheena, Queen of the Jungle*—all these comics were violently racist and very sadistic. Most of the evildoers in them were Japanese, rather than German, though the stray Nazi might appear.

I read these comics with shock, but I didn't really become interested in comics until I was an adult, investigating the Yellow Peril panic, which in essence had the Mongol Horde riding again. The various Fu Manchu movies starring Christopher Lee are modern-day Yellow Perilism; and our current worries about being crushed by China's economic might is an extension of the syndrome. I am lucky to own the key Yellow Peril book, M. P. Shiel's *The Yellow Danger,* as well as a lot of truly goofy stuff published in California in the late nineteenth century. In pulp fiction, movies, television, Wall Street, and the business pages—indeed, throughout our popular culture—the Yellow Peril is still very much with us, and probably always will be.

7

ARCHER CITY, AT the time we moved in from the ranch, was an oil-patch town of perhaps twelve hundred souls. It opened, on all sides, back into the country. One might think that living in a small house on the edge of town, with a hay field between it and Mr. Will Taylor's mansion, was not very different from living in the country, in a ranch house eighteen miles from town.

One would be wrong to assume that, though. In the country we were a more or less self-sufficient group, and were still directed, to a large extent, by the implacable will of my grandmother, Louisa Francis McMurtry. One of the reasons *The Swiss Family Robinson* has long been a favorite of mine—in childhood I read it many times—is that I identified with the hard-pressed but resourceful Robinsons.* We too were hard-pressed, but resourceful. My grandmother still made her own soap. We had a huge garden; we never had to buy vegetables from a store. We butchered our own beef, and likewise our own pork. We ate our chickens, with now and then a guinea hen or turkey for variety.

For playmates I had my cousins John K. and Mary Louise. We didn't have to deal with anacondas, as the Robinsons did, but as I have mentioned, rattlers were plentiful.

---

*Oddly, to this day, I've never been able to read either *Robinson Crusoe* or—the real source of both books—Alexander Selkirk's account of his own shipwreck and stranding.

Country existence, in the 1940s, was a kind of *Swiss Family Robinson* existence. Both the deep freeze and the pressure cooker came into common use about this time, making self-sufficiency even easier. Though the pressure cooker proved to be a tricky appliance—explosions were not infrequent—nevertheless hundreds of jars of corn, peaches, tomatoes, green beans, cabbage, and pickles began to accumulate on shelves my father built in the cellar.

8

DESPITE ALL THESE improvements in country living, we *did* move to town, and the change from country to village life had profound significance for me. In the country I had done a lot of imagining, most of it inspired by radio. In town I soon had half a dozen playmates, all of them living more or less on our block.

The Tarzan movies that starred Johnny Weissmuller were at the height of their popularity just then—my new playmates and I became, for a time, so many Tarzans and Janes.

Our move to town occurred in 1943, when I would have been in the second grade. The school curriculum was not rigorous. I went to the Archer City school for twelve years and cannot remember ever taking home a textbook. Much as I loved reading, I didn't love reading textbooks. Longfellow was perhaps the hardest poet we were ever made to read, and Poe and Irving probably the most advanced prose writers. School was something all children had to do, and there had to be teachers to teach them, but anything resembling a passion for learning was not to be found in Archer City and pretty much still isn't, I fear.

There was then no public library in Archer City—I eventually helped start one twenty years later—but as an A student, I was allowed free run of the small school library, though it was supposed to be for high-schoolers. It contained a shabby collection of once-popular fiction. I read the longest book in it, *Gone With the Wind,* and much later, in *Lonesome Dove,* produced what I consider to be the *Gone With the Wind* of the West; but somehow, I could never get interested in the tragedies of the South, even though I had an uncle on my mother's side, the redoubtable Jeff Dobbs, who to his dying day cursed the memory of William Tecumseh Sherman.

Jeff Dobbs happened to be at Fort Sill when Geronimo was captive there. It startled him that the Apaches and Comanches, once given their allotment of beef, immediately gutted the beeves and offered their children slices of the intestines, as we might offer our children chocolate.

Later, once his wife—my aunt Minta—was killed in a car wreck, Jeff Dobbs grew bored with cooking and ate his meat raw.

In my senior year, by then obsessed with books, I stole a few from the high school library, mostly very cheap editions of books that were supposed to be classics: Addison and Steele, for example. The teachers observed this but they didn't stop me. I was a kind of special case. While on our senior trip to Colorado City the teachers crept into my room and took the books back. Nothing was ever said about this, but I felt a little better about myself when Susan Sontag told me that she had sometimes taken a bus from North Hollywood to steal Modern Library books from the great Pickwick Bookshop, on Hollywood Boulevard.

There was a time when, like Susan, I *had* to have books. Once I reached driving age I often spent Sunday afternoons driving the dirt roads of Archer County, looking for abandoned farmhouses. These were not hard to find—many farms had failed during the Dust Bowl years. Now and then I would find a few books in those houses—they weren't much, but I was firmly started on my book hunting.

I have handled, as a bookseller, at least a million volumes, and I am still buying books both new and old. The fun now comes in happening on an important or exciting book that I have never owned or, perhaps, have never read. First one has to find such a book; then one has to recognize it for what it is.

9

As I HAVE noted, I took a look at the comics in the local drugstore but I didn't spend many of my dimes buying them. I did not "collect" comics then, though when my grandson Curtis McMurtry was in his early teens I did encourage him to "collect" comics and graphic novels and, in fact, watched him form a good collection both of Silver Age and post-*RAW* comics.* There is a healthy comics culture in Austin, where Curtis lives, and many, indeed most, of our visits involved taking Curtis to the best comics store in town, where he was—and is—a respected customer.

Much later, in my forties and fifties, I did become interested in comics on an international scale, both because of their deeply pervasive sadism and because of their frequent borrowings from earlier comic artists. By chance I was in Rome for several weeks in 1973, being a stage dad while my son James acted in Peter Bogdanovich's *Daisy Miller*. James played Daisy's rambunctious brother, Randolph.

Having nothing to do all day I walked and walked around Rome. One day, near the railroad station, I stumbled on some book stalls where they sold used Italian comic books. These were the famous *fumetti noir*, which, in the sixties and early seventies, were fairly restrained: no pubic hair, no overt sex. By the early eighties these *fumetti* became openly and often

---

RAW is the magazine where many of today's dark-visioned comics artists (Art Spiegelman, Dan Clowes, and others) made their home.

grotesquely pornographic. Their heroines were based on then-famous actresses: Brigitte Bardot ("Isabella"), Senta Berger ("Jungla"), Ursula Andress (in a James Bond rip-off called *Goldrake*), and so on.

What arrested me, at first glance, were the many similarities in these violent comics to the Fiction House comics of the forties and fifties.

I bought a lot of the *fumetti* and sent them home. Later, reflecting on how rare these trivial publications would become over time, I commissioned two friends, poets both, to journey from Venice to Naples just to buy me *fumetti*. They went, and in Naples were rewarded by the discovery of the Supermarket del Fumetto, where they bought me hundreds of comics and shipped them to Brooklyn, from whose difficult port I had some trouble extracting them, though I eventually succeeded.

Thus the history of my involvement with the international comics movement belongs not to my youth but to my middle age. In my fifties I bought the whole catalogue of an Oregon distributor called Fantagraphics. This purchase—not expensive in today's terms—brought me most of what was good in modern comic art, as well as subscriptions to several scholarly magazines devoted to comics. Some of these magazines are still trickling in.

I tried for several years to keep abreast of advancing developments in France, Italy, Spain, and our own underground comics scene, which began, as nearly as I can tell—this is sure to be disputed—with a sheet called *Yellow Dog,* out of Austin, Texas.

In the seventies the French began publishing very expensive hardback comics, whose price might run as high as $50 each. The Italians and the Spanish soon followed suit. These comics, attractive at first, soon became erotica, pure and simple: Guido Crepax illustrating *The Story of O,* or the famous *Click* series of Milo Manara. I didn't disapprove of the erotica, but I balked at the price. Of fifty-dollar comics I had enough, already.

I O

BY CHANCE, IN the sixties, I bought, from a paperback exchange in San Antonio, a big pile of pre-code Fiction House comics. There were more than 150 of them; they had belonged to an airman who suddenly needed money. I took the lot for $1 a comic. One day, in the dream time of my age, I meant to compare the Fiction House comics of the forties and early fifties with the *fumetti noir* of the sixties and early seventies, perhaps throwing in a few of the high-end French comics, to see if I could make an essay, or maybe a whole book, about the country-to-country migration of comic motifs: it would be something like what Aby Warburg once did with ornamental motifs in architecture.

In the late 1940s and early 1950s the American comic book industry came under heavy attack from two critics, one famous and powerful, the other obscure. Of the two, the obscure one, G. Legman, was by far the more brilliant: his *Love and Death* (Breaking Point, 1949) was as fine a polemic as America has produced, if America produced it. I'd put it up there with *Common Sense*.

I will have more to say about the gifted G. Legman a little later. Despite the death-thrust nature of his attack, *Love and Death* got little attention, although the critic Leslie Fiedler certainly read it and sprang from it into his *Love and Death in the American Novel.*

The comics industry never heard of Legman, but they certainly heard about their more visible adversary, Dr. Fredric Wertham, who called his well-documented attack on the comic book industry *Seduction of the Innocent* (1954).

Dr. Wertham argued, pretty effectively, that a steady diet of extreme visual sadism might permanently unsettle young minds. Of course, a few kids did damage themselves trying to fly like Superman, or by doing violence to their friends or victims.

Dr. Wertham's forceful attack was not ignored, as Legman's had been. The furor got the attention of those in high places, including members of Congress.

The comic publishers proceeded to panic—many of them probably had no idea what fiendish stuff their artists were turning out week after week. When they did look, forced to by Dr. Wertham, they were horrified—or maybe they were merely horrified by the sudden drop in their share prices. In any case they quickly offered to censor themselves, the Comics Code was born, and the Golden Age of American comics ended. (*Spider-Man* and the *Hulk* are Silver Age.) There was still violence, of course, but it was seldom sexually tinted, as it had been during the Golden Age.

The only Silver Age comics I have any use for are the funny ones: *Mad, Uncle Scrooge, Pogo,* and the famous *Shmoo* book of Al Capp.

It was rumored, but not, so far as I know, proven, that Al Capp (creator of *L'il Abner*) hid pornographic elements in some of his panels, those to be enjoyed by the select few who were in the know. A watch chain might droop like a penis, or whatever.

I don't know about the pornographic panels, but I do know that comics artists are not infrequently weird. The movie *Crumb*, about the comics artist R. Crumb (*Fritz the Cat* and much else), supports this view, while being the single most depressing movie I have ever seen.

II

THE GREAT REVOLUTION in the world of books and reading—immediately noticeable even in Archer City—was the paperback revolution. The paperbacks arrived just in time for me to view—but not buy—the famous cover of Mickey Spillane's *I, the Jury,* in which an evil "real blonde" is in the process of taking off her clothes. She is trying to save her life by seducing Mike Hammer, Mickey Spillane's trademark detective, but sadly, the ploy doesn't work. Mike Hammer shoots her in the stomach, and that's that.

The next Mickey Spillane I remember seeing in the drugstore was *One Lonely Night,* which shows Mike's beautiful secretary, Velda, hanging naked from a rope and being beaten by Nazis. We don't actually see the Nazis, whom Mike Hammer promptly kills.

I didn't purchase that one either, though I believe I soon picked up both volumes secondhand. The paperback revolution had barely started when paperback exchanges arrived a step behind; people would trade two of their already-read paperbacks for one they hadn't read. Paperback exchanges continue to thrive in many cities. Our bookshop, Booked Up, once supplied two, one in Laguna, New Mexico, and another in Worland, Wyoming.

In those adolescent days I read what I could scrounge. When my father attended to weekly livestock auctions in Wichita Falls I would sometimes drop off in town and make the rounds of newsstands and secondhand furniture stores, where a few books were sometimes to be found.

I also began to visit Lovelace's Bookshop, on Indiana Street. It was a very friendly store that, nonetheless, scared me for a time. I didn't feel educated enough to be in a real bookshop—even a modest one such as Lovelace's clearly was. It was there that I saw my first Modern Library book; Lovelace's stocked a shelf or two of books that were considered classics, books I regarded with a mixture of awe and fear. Most of them featured authors, or even languages, that I had never heard of.

At that time I only vaguely knew that there was a language called Latin and a language called Greek, and I doubt that I knew about Russian yet.

On my first few visits to Lovelace's I don't think I bought anything, which the kindly staff did not seem to hold against me. Encouraged, I finally did buy a book, *Madame Bovary.* It had a faux-leather spine and belonged to an inexpensive set of classics that were like the Modern Library, though in this case *not* the Modern Library.

12

THROUGH THE YEARS of my late childhood and early adolescence my parents seemed mildly surprised that I liked to read so much, but they didn't *mind* that I read a lot, and they exhibited no interest at all in what I might be reading. They took no notice of my little *Madame Bovary,* and yet, somehow, I think they might have taken notice if I'd showed up with *I, the Jury.* I *did* read the Spillane books, of course, and my parents (who, after all, had three younger children to deal with) would probably not quite have known what they were objecting to, had it occurred to them to object.

When I was about nine we ceased to have a cook and I moved into the tiny, freezing garage apartment that the cook had been inhabiting. I didn't mind that the garage was freezing: the privacy was worth it, and the actual house was bursting at the seams anyway, with my parents and (soon) three siblings crammed into it.

Mickey Spillane was a mediocre detective writer, and yet the famous paperback cover of that "real blonde" in a sense pointed the way to the vast loosening of sexual morals that occurred in America and Western Europe in the 1960s.

Rather rapidly, not far down the road, was the *Lady Chatterley* trial, Henry Miller, *Howl,* Flower Power, the Rolling Stones, and so on. Paperback covers, many very sexy, were the advance guard of the rapid breakdown of sexual restraint among the middle classes almost everywhere. The cover of *I, the Jury* was mild indeed compared to many that would come.

13

BY THE MID-SIXTIES the bookseller in me awoke to the fact that those early mass market paperbacks—they're now called "vintage" paperbacks—would become salable very soon. There would be people collecting them, a prediction almost immediately confirmed.

So I quickly made a plan: I would assemble first printings of the first five hundred titles from the first five mass market paperback houses, and those would be Pocket Books (the most staid), Dell (famous for its mapback mysteries), Popular Library, Avon (the best covers), and Gold Medal originals (the least staid). The hardboiled writer Jim Thompson published some of his work—*Texas by the Tail* and *South of Heaven*—with Gold Medal, hard-to-come-by titles today and, when come by, expensive.

Fortunately I knew just where to go to form my baseline collection of American mass market paperbacks, and that was Harper's, in the area known as Deep Ellum, in Dallas, Texas.

Lloyd Harper and his wife and son ran a big general bookshop in Deep Ellum, which, to this day, is not rock-solid safe. Mr. Harper had the largest stock of secondhand paperbacks anywhere in the Southwest. Most of them were stacked in vast piles on his cavernous second floor. Many of these came from a first-look deal he had with either the local Goodwill or the local Salvation Army or both. This deal yielded many thousands of magazines, paperbacks, and books, not a few of which were good.

I told Mr. Harper what I had in mind and he kindly gave me permission to find what I could in his upstairs. My recollection is that I got about twelve hundred paperbacks on my first sweep, which put me about halfway to my goal of twenty-five hundred volumes, which would represent the first five hundred publications of the first five big-time paperback houses.

It was a start, and naturally I augmented it by scouting the paperback exchanges in Houston, where I was then teaching. Paperback scouting is ideal work for impecunious young professors, which is what I then was. I scouted often and covered lots of ground.

Soon, though, book selling claimed more and more of my attention, and academia less. My son James was then seven, and thus fairly easily movable. I left Rice thinking I would return, but I didn't return. Instead my son James and I settled into the hamlet of Waterford, in northern Virginia, where we lived until James left for college.

The paperback collection got moved to Virginia and, in Virginia, moved several more times as we changed houses. The collection came to seem like a collection that would never be unpacked.

A friend of ours, Greg Curtis, then the editor in chief of *Texas Monthly*, relieved himself of the tensions of editorship by going to garage sales around Austin, where, mainly, he scouted for records. At some point, though, vintage paperbacks began to catch his eye. Soon he was trading for early paperbacks, and remembered my collection, which eventually I sold to him, feeling that I would probably never see the likes of those pristine copies again.

In fact I did see their likes again. A dealer in Wichita Falls made a big paperback purchase, and was happy to sell the vintage stuff to me. These numbered several hundred books, and contained at least eighty percent of the titles I sold to Greg. When Booked Up purchased Barber's Bookstore, in Fort Worth, I siphoned off a few hundred more, all of which now ring the shelves of what once, long ago, was Mr. Will Taylor's servants' quarters, a plain two-story brick house which we nicknamed the Petit Trianon.

I seldom study or refer to those paperbacks now, but I'm nonetheless glad I have them, because I can pull almost any one of them off the shelf and be reminded of how life was in the late forties and the early fifties. They help me remember that moment when I walked into the old drugstore in Archer City and picked up that copy of *I, the Jury:* then I realized only dimly that times were changing, but change they did.

14

My schooling in the Archer City public school was a social, rather than an educative, experience. It lasted twelve years and then, abruptly, it ended. I was out on the street, graduated, along with the other eighteen members of my class.

Before I graduated, I can't remember that much, if any, thought had been given as to where I would go to college. There was a university just twenty miles away, Midwestern State University, in Wichita Falls. It was a rather attractive school, architecturally, at least, but I had no desire to go there.

If I went anywhere—and there was no certainty that I would—I wanted to be farther from home.

In this era of early admissions such a lack of interest in higher education on my parents' part seems incredible; but there it was. What made it more strange was that my father had actually graduated from a college: Clarendon College, in Clarendon (Donley County), Texas. The McMurtrys old and young had clustered around Clarendon for a time in the twenties, but the old folks got homesick for Archer County; they went home and my father went with them, but not before attending this prairie school for two years.

I only discovered this fact when I acquired a book about the school and discovered my father's name in the graduating class of 1922. I think he may have once or twice mentioned that he had attended college, but he didn't particularize it. So far as I remember, the only evidence of his college education was that he often quoted the famous Polonius line from *Hamlet:* "Neither a borrower nor a lender be."

Unfortunately my father had to be a borrower for at least fifty-five straight years: cheap bank credit was all that saved him as a rancher. He was also, on occasion, a lender.

I think my father may have vaguely entertained the notion that I should skip college and help him run the ranch. If he did entertain this notion, he soon dismissed it. By the time I was eighteen I had worked with him a lot—enough to make him painfully aware that, while I was passable on a horse, I entirely lacked manual skills. I can still barely put a ribbon in this typewriter. Since most of ranching involves the application of manual skills—fence building, for example—a total lack of them was a serious limitation.

My mother took little interest in this selection process—really, a non-selection process. I think she supposed that I would break down and go to Midwestern—thus, in effect, staying home, which was precisely what I didn't want to do.

My father then had the worst idea of all, which was that I go to Texas A&M and become a vet. A vet? Me? I regarded most animals as my enemies and had no particular sensitivity to them. Why would I want to spend my life healing them?

I'm not sure why my father made that suggestion, which, had it been adopted, would have been a mistake of epic proportion. Probably he just reasoned that good vets were in short supply—ergo, I would have a job.

Yet weird as it seems, that could have happened—or at least part of it, the A&M part—could have happened. I would never have made it far in vet school. Nonetheless, for a month or so, I supposed I was destined for A&M (although I hadn't applied there, or indeed anywhere).

I was saved from this only by the happy accident of sitting down in front of our new TV and watching a program about Rice Institute (now University) in Houston. The campus had what I supposed to be an Oxford-like look—actually the architecture was partly Moorish, and I, of course, had never been to the real Oxford then, but the program pointed out that the school was organized on a college system, like the real Oxford.

But best of all, Rice was free—if one could get in. My parents liked the idea of free. A sticking point was that acceptance required a face-to-face interview. My parents were not keen on taking me to Houston, four hundred miles away, for this interview, but they took me. They liked the campus and so did I, but someone in the admissions department noted that my math stopped at Algebra II, whereas freshman math at Rice started with calculus.

I was initially rejected, but was put on a waiting list and, at the last moment, got in. I went, but knew at once that my stay in Houston would be temporary: the highest grade I ever got in a math class was 4.

15

THIS IS A book about my life with books, not a book about my schooling. Where books come into it is that I spent the year and a half that constituted my first stay at Rice—there would be three—in the wonderful open-stack Fondren Library, which contained, at that time, about six hundred thousand volumes: heaven! I was, to say the least, thrilled, and when I went back to Rice as a graduate student and, later, a professor, I still spent much of my time wandering around Fondren. I spent so much time walking the stacks that I soon had a good visual sense of how the subjects were shelved, and what was there.

I later romanticized Fondren and my relationship with it in a book called *All My Friends Are Going to Be Strangers,* in which my young hero, Danny Deck, mainly sleeps on the comfortable couches in Fondren, from which he is sometimes routed by a librarian named Dame Juliana, after Dame Juliana of Norwich.

Actually, I never slept in that library, since my $15-a-month apartment was only a five-minute walk.

Lately Rice graciously offered to name a reading room after me and I ungraciously declined, my grounds being that having things named after me makes me feel posthumous.

The well-stocked reference section of this library was just to the right as one walked in. Something deep inside me must already have been preparing for my career as a bookman, because I soon found that I was paying more attention to the bibliography than I was to the literature itself.

This habit to an extent continues. From the moment I considered being an antiquarian book seller I began to assemble a reference library, now containing several thousand volumes. I have complete runs of both the British and the American book auction records, plus Sabin and the British Museum catalogue and hundreds of author bibliographies. Even so my reference library is modest, never rivaling that of great dealers such as Warren Howell or H. P. Kraus. The latter had a whole floor, in his seven-story building at 16 East Forty-sixth Street in New York, devoted entirely to reference. The Kraus reference books went into the salesrooms and are now dispersed.

There have been dealers I've known who have more reference books than they have books for sale. The late Franklin Gilliam of the Brick Row Book Shop was one such, and there are plenty of others. Knowing what there is to know about a given book can be more fun than merely selling it.

Most young dealers of the Silicon Chip Era regard a reference library as merely a waste of space. Old-timers on the West Coast, such as Peter Howard of Serendipity Books in Berkeley or Lou and Ben Weinstein of the (recently closed) Heritage Book Shop in Los Angeles, seem to retain a fondness for reference books that goes beyond the practical. Everything there is to know about a given volume may be only a click away, but there are still a few of us who'd rather have the book than the click. A bookman's love of books is a love of *books,* not merely of the information in them.

16
___

ONE MIGHT POSE this question: If you don't enjoy the physical work of handling books, why be an antiquarian book seller at all? There are certainly better ways to make money than selling secondhand books. The pleasure of a hands-on approach to book selling is both intellectual and tactile. The best bookmen rarely lose or exhaust their curiosity about editions, variants, points, bindings, provenance, cost codes, and the like. The things there are to know about a given book—particularly if it's a complicated book, with a complicated text—absorb the attention of the best dealers for a lifetime. And certainly a normal lifetime is not long enough to enable one to learn even half of what there is to know about antiquarian books in general.

I myself, for example, once sold a book worth several thousand dollars for $45 to a next-door dealer who had already passed on it several times. It was *Les Jeux de la poupée,* the famous tortured-doll book done by the Belgian surrealist Hans Bellmer, which I foolishly took for a mere exhibition catalogue. It was in part of a collection of several thousand exhibition catalogues we had purchased from the estate of a man long prominent in the Washington museum world. I had grown bored with pricing these five- and ten-dollar catalogues, and yet, when I picked up the Bellmer, I had the vague feeling that this was something different. How many times do you see exhibitions of dolls wrapped in barbed wire?

I set the item aside for more mature consideration, but I never gave it more mature consideration. Instead I sold it to the handiest willing dealer, for $45 less 20 percent. The dealer, who had a shop across the street, boldly priced it at $120—a Boston dealer grabbed it, and when next heard of, it was on sale for $5,000. An inscribed copy is in the auction rooms now: estimate $60,000 to $80,000.

I don't really regret that error. No dealer can know everything, and when a shop such as Booked Up yields up a great sleeper, the word gets out and the scouts and dealers come running. They won't find anything on the order of the Bellmer, but they will buy something anyway.

All dealers tend to remember the books that they see only once. Only one or two of my own books are in any sense rare, and those are in fact pamphlets.

A dealer in the sixties, annoyed by the claims made for books that were in no sense rare, issued a catalogue called *Uncommon Rare Books.* I'm not sure the trade was especially amused.

17

ONCE I ACCEPTED that Math 100 was a hurdle I was never going to clear, I put my mind at rest and felt free to explore Houston, my first city and one I still love, in part for its hustle and its welcoming spirit. There is graft and fraud in abundance—witness Enron. But Enron is only one corrupt player among many, present and past.

Since I had no car, my first problem was to master the city bus system, which I did with ease. When I was back at Rice as a graduate student in 1958, I casually bused across the nearly all-black Fifth Ward in order to teach night school at the University of Houston, an urban university that seemed a world away from the tranquil purlieus of Rice.

I was never harassed on a Houston city bus, although I was often the only white person on the bus. But I was constantly harassed by my students at night school, many of whom were cops who failed to see the virtues of *Beowulf* or Dylan Thomas. I was widely disliked because—idealist that I then was—I expected the students to read their assignments. Since few did, I sometimes resorted to reading the assigned text aloud. This was not welcome but it *was* soporific. Generally about half of my class fell dead asleep.

Meanwhile I developed complete confidence in the Houston public transportation system, as well as in my own ability to navigate it.

Fortunately, for a time all three of Houston's main secondhand book stores were downtown, reachable without even changing buses. The dean of Houston booksellers, to the extent that there was one at that time, was Herbert Fletcher, whose shop, though not really grand, was grand enough to intimidate me. Later Mr. Fletcher retired to the hill town of Salado, where he and (I believe) his son ran a book barn from which I occasionally bought books.

Easily the most colorful of the Houston booksellers was the elegant, irascible Ted Brown, who made a fortune selling technical books to the oil and petrochemical companies that—once air-conditioning reached Houston—lined the Ship Channel. Ted's shop was not really antiquarian, but he always kept a wall of fancy books, first editions, bindings, and press books for his rich customers from River Oaks and the Memorial district, where Ted himself lived.

I naturally gravitated to the fancy books and have to this day a lovely two-volume nineteenth-century *Anatomy of Melancholy,* in calf with morocco labels, which I acquired for $7.50. It's the earliest-acquired book in my library, and I purchased it despite Ted Brown's acerbic disapproval.

I always liked looking at Ted's carriage-trade books. In 1958 or so, when I was back at Rice as a graduate student (the shame of Math 100 long forgotten), I picked up and examined the signed, limited edition of William Faulkner's *A Fable.* "You can't afford that," Ted insisted, taking it out of my hand. At the time he was right: I couldn't afford it. This was in fact merely byplay; Ted liked me and later gave me two autograph parties.

When Ted Brown died I owned a small bookshop on Studemont Street, in what Houstonians call the Heights. Once a haven for old-money Houstonians, and boasting some fine Edwardian mansions, the Heights had become a barrio. When Ted died, we were invited to bid on his library, but I had just had quadruple bypass surgery in Baltimore and was too sick to be hustling books. Cured in the flesh but far from well in spirit, I made a trip to Houston just to see what Ted Brown had acquired.

He had a decent library, but several of my own early books, inscribed to him, were the most expensive things in it. We made a nominal bid and let it go. The signed, limited *Fable* was still there. I couldn't afford it and no one else wanted it, so Ted Brown took it home.

18

THE THIRD SECONDHAND bookshop in downtown Houston in the fifties was run by a nice, rumpled man named Joe Petty. General urban second-hand bookstores have a way of making their owners look rumpled. One reason I'm comfortable in dusty bookshops is that I have no sartorial interests. As I may have mentioned in an earlier book, *Walter Benjamin at the Dairy Queen,* the only books I can remember buying at Joe Petty's bookshop, on my first pass at least, were by the Frenchman Romain Rolland. Why him? Didn't he win the Nobel Prize? If so, why?

I have long since got rid of the Romain Rolland but may still have a volume or two of the attractive edition of Proust published in the thirties by Albert and Charles Boni.

By this time in the late fifties I had become alert to the possibility of finding desirable books in charity stores and junk shops. My two favorites were the big Goodwill store on Washington Avenue—chancy territory then, as it still is—and Trash and Treasure, on Westheimer, which was more or less in walking distance of where James and I lived. The best book I ever found at Trash and Treasure was *The Fugitive Anthology,* which I got for a buck. It was an anthology of the poetry of the once stiff-necked Southern agrarians: Tate, Ransom, Donald Davidson, and, improbably, Laura Riding.

I'm aware that this kind of prattle is exactly the kind of prattle I ought to be avoiding, lest this become a narrative that is of interest only to bookmen. The model for such books is *The Compleat Angler:* oh look, I caught a First Folio today.

It's best, then, to emphasize that at this period I was seeking books that I wanted to *read*—not sell. Psychologically at least, selling was a long way ahead. I have recorded elsewhere that I left a track meet in Fort Worth, took a downtown bus, and visited Barber's Book Store, where I bought a book by Hugh Walpole called *Rogue Herries.*

About forty years later I caught the then owner of Barber's Book Store, Bryan Perkins, in a selling mood, so I bought the whole bookshop, seventeen Hertz Penske trucks full, thus acquiring several more titles by Hugh Walpole, all of them still unread.

When freshman math finally squeezed me out of Rice I fell back on North Texas State College (now North Texas University), in Denton, now a suburb both of Dallas and Fort Worth. There is still a little bit of green between Denton and Fort Worth, but no green at all between Denton and Dallas.

From the first, Denton's one big draw for me was the excellent bus service between Denton and Dallas, giving me access to the Dallas bookshops. Besides Harper's, where I spent a lot of time, there was a dim cave near the bus station run by the old, nearly toothless Mr. Moses, whose books were very cheap.

I also did my best, in this period, to make myself acceptable to the one modestly high-end dealer in Dallas, the redoubtable Sawnie Aldredge, dealer to the Dallas carriage trade, such as it was—at the time I met Sawnie the carriage trade seemed a little thin, forcing Sawnie, like any other dealer, to sell what he could find to anyone who wanted to buy it.

Certainly he always sold books to me merrily enough, whenever I showed up, which was whenever I had $20 to spare. The last time I visited Sawnie I bought a lovely copy of *The Great Gatsby,* in a fine dust wrapper (issue then unknown), for the modest price of $12. It was priced $15, but Sawnie had already accepted me as a proto-dealer, and courteously gave me the customary discount.

This copy of *Gatsby* slowly migrated upward. My spirited and acute book selling partner Marcia Carter, who ran the Georgetown Booked Up for thirty-two years, discovered that her back porch needed urgent repair, so she sold the *Gatsby* to Joseph the Provider, in Santa Barbara. I don't know where that *Gatsby* is now but a copy that looked something like it was sold by Christie's in the Robert Rechler sale, in 2003, where it made $120,000. Another fine copy has since gone as high as $168,000, which is a lot more than $12.

I happened to buy that *Gatsby* just at the moment when the most sought-after moderns began their spectacular rise. It's now forty years later and they're still going up.

This may be somehow related to the fact that America, according to *The New York Times,* now has 946 billionaires. Yipes! and yipes! again. I can remember when there were only the Hunts, Getty, Daniel Ludwig, and a few others in the billionaire class. With nearly a thousand billionaires running around, it's no wonder that the value of pricey rarities has risen so spectacularly, and probably will continue to.

19

FOR THE FIRST twenty years of my career as a book hunter I actually *read* almost all the books I had gone to such trouble to find. Getting the books I wanted to read was the main reason for the pursuit.

But there can be secondary and tertiary reasons for wanting a particular book. One is the pleasure of holding the physical book itself: savoring the type, the binding, the book's feel and heft. All these things can be enjoyed apart from literature, which some, but not all, books contain.

For a while bibliography seduced me. I acquired Jacob Blanck's *American First Editions* and lost myself, for a time, in the intricacies of issues, points, cancels, colophons, and the rest.

I also, perversely, kept buying French literature that was at the time over my head. I think I just liked the foreignness of it. Somewhere, possibly at Lovelace's, I discovered the Heritage Club, which issued nicely made but inexpensive reprints of various classics—what the Folio Society, in England, did and did better. The first Heritage Club book to reach me was Anatole France's *Penguin Island,* of which I read perhaps three pages.

The first literary critic I can recall reading was an English journalist who called himself Solomon Eagle, and who wrote hundreds of light essays of a bookish nature for a great variety of London magazines. I bought a book of his called *Books in General* and read it several times.

Solomon Eagle was in fact a rather lightweight English man of letters named J. C. Squire. There are at least two series of *Books in General*—in time I acquired a respectable shelf of the now forgotten J. C. Squire, who was decidely not a modernist. He was a big fan of Dr. Johnson and a savage enemy of James Joyce. For a time he had some power in the London literary world—he even edited the *London Mercury*. When a review copy of *Ulysses* reached him—and there weren't many review copies of *Ulysses* sent out—Squire flung it in the fireplace, from which, fortunately, it was saved by a young editor who had better sense than his boss.

For a time, in my bibliographical period, I became absorbed with issue points, on the order of the famous "stoppped" on page 81, line 26, of Hemingway's *The Sun Also Rises*. Even at my sickest, after heart surgery, I could remember that point and a few others, when I could remember little else.

As the high spots of modern literature soar in value, more and more issue points have been discovered, many of them on the dust wrappers, rather than the books themselves. For big-ticket books such as *The Maltese Falcon, The Great Gatsby,* or *The Sound and the Fury,* the first-issue dust wrapper is far harder to obtain than the first-issue book.

Beginning to try to make literature—or even, when faced with the likes of Joyce, Proust, and Stein, just trying to read it—was a huge challenge. I had no more background from which to approach those writers than I had in approaching the calculus. I never heard of any of them until I got to college, nor did I, for a time, hear much of them at Rice, where many of the professors, particularly the older ones, held attitudes toward modernism that were not so different from J. C. Squire's.

20

In 1959 I married Jo Ballard Scott, of Florence, South Carolina. Jo spent our marriage reading Proust and Gibbon. Proust she read in French, in the Pléiade edition.

That was fine with me. I was happy to have a wife who read Proust and Gibbon, rather than, say, *Ladies' Home Journal.*

Jo came to the end of those great works about the time we came to the end of our marriage, though we weren't divorced or even widely separated for several more years.

When I graduated from North Texas State, where I met Jo, then a student at Texas Woman's University, across town (Denton), I took a week off from helping my father on the ranch to begin a novel, which eventually became *Horseman, Pass By* (1961). My method of writing a novel was, from the first, to get up early and dash off five pages of narrative. That is still my method, though now I dash off ten pages a day. I write every day, ignoring holidays and weekends.

I wrote on and on, deep into summer. I finished a draft of *Horseman* and continued right on into a second novel, which I called *Memories of the Old Tribe,* about a rancher, a cowboy, and the woman they both loved. By October of 1958, back at Rice to do graduate work, I had, in draft, two novels.

I was studying for a doctorate in English, but I didn't have to get it, and the reason I didn't was that I had the energy to get up early and write those five pages. Soon I had fiction to show; instead of learning German and Old English, I used my manuscripts to get a fellowship in the Wallace Stegner Fellowship class at Stanford University. I settled for an M.A. at Rice, and a few more weeks of cowboying with my father, before Jo and I and our dog, Putnam, set off for the fabled West Coast.

We routed ourselves through Denver, where I book scouted while Jo and Putnam frolicked in a park. All I bought in Denver was the attractive two-volume Oxford Montaigne, translated by Trechmann. I visited the somewhat crusty Mr. Dan Block but couldn't afford his books, and I didn't even attempt to invade the sanctum of Mr. Fred Rosenstock, then the dean of Denver booksellers.

Once in the Bay Area we settled into a little house in a cornfield in Palo Alto, a stone's throw from the 101 Freeway, the road that would eventually take me south to Hollywood.

The story of our time at Stanford has been told already, in *Walter Benjamin at the Dairy Queen.* In this narrative I'll skip Stanford and get right to the bookshops.

In Palo Alto–Menlo Park I remember two. The famously grouchy Mr. Bell in Palo Alto ordered me off his second floor, although I had a book in my hand and I bought it! It was *Annals of English Literature,* a book useful to graduate students for its precise listing of birth dates, death dates, and publication dates for English writers.

The other peninsular bookseller I remember was William Wreden, who then operated from a gracious house on the edge of Menlo Park. Over the years—thirty or more—I bought books from Mr. Wreden many times, and late in the nineties, I ended up with hundreds of scraps from his stock, sold me by Peter Howard and Ian Jackson, both of Berkeley, who bought what was left of Mr. Wreden's stock from his estate.

Once, in my student days, I offered Mr. Wreden a pile of local fine printing acquired at a library sale, and he paid me well—and could afford to. His family, I was told, owned the second biggest ranch in California. That he had money caused him to be resented by some of his less lucky competitors, notably the magisterial Warren Howell, of whom more later.

William Wreden was always kind to me, and he always had interesting books, which is the highest compliment one bookseller can pay another. At the various book fairs that were soon springing up, Mr. Wreden could be seen busily selling pamphlets, of which he had many thousands. And many of his pamphlets can now be found on the north wall of Booked Up's Building Three, in Archer City.

Jo and I both found Palo Alto charmless, so, after a few weeks, we moved into the city of San Francisco.

2 1

I DUTIFULLY DID my five pages every day; Jo worked for Crown Zeller-bach; Putnam brooded until one of us came home to what was then called a pad, on Clay Street, and took him for a walk.

Once my writing duty was done each morning, I went out into the city and spent the rest of my day in bookstores.

The rest of the day and often some of the night: San Francisco was not Peoria. Businesses, including bookshops, often stayed open much of the night.

I don't think I had ever heard the term "book scout" until, one night, I wandered into the Discovery Bookstore, in North Beach, and met the poet David Meltzer, who sometimes ran the shop at night.

Discovery was right next door to the more famous City Lights book-shop; both shops stayed open well past midnight.

I had, by this time, drawn up a list of books I couldn't find and *really* wanted to read. A list, in other words, of desiderata—later in life I saw such a list that had been issued by G. Legman, he of *Love and Death,* from La Clé des Champs, Valbonne, Alpes-Maritimes, France. Legman's wants were mostly folkloristic in nature, but mine were not. First on my list was *Let Us Now Praise Famous Men,* by James Agee with pictures by Walker Evans—this work was soon to be reprinted and is now easy to get.

The second book I sought, and asked David to find, was Legman's searing polemic *Love and Death,* which I have already mentioned. To my astonishment David produced a copy the very next day, and the copy he produced was even more unusual than even he may have realized. *Love and Death* is a short book, usually found in red-and-black wrappers. But the copy I purchased was hardbound *and* inscribed. I still have it, and it remains the only hardbound copy I have ever seen.

When I had come to know G. Legman a little bit—through correspondence, at first—I asked him about the binding of my copy, which looks very much like a New Directions binding. Legman said that James Laughlin, the publisher of New Directions, had considered taking on *Love and Death* but in the end decided not to.

Since both men were famously grumpy, it is little wonder that *Love and Death* was not published by New Directions.

22

I SOON TOOK to dropping in at the Discovery Bookstore every night or so, and David Meltzer and I quickly became friends. One day he even asked me to go scouting with him in the East Bay. I knew little of book scouting but I did have one asset David lacked: a car. Soon we were off.

This, I believe, was pre-Serendipity, but not by much. Peter Howard would soon be operating out of a warren of shops on Shattuck Avenue; but David directed me first to Oakland, and to downtown Oakland at that—it was then still rather *Grapes of Wrath*–ish, with many drifters on the streets.

Our first destination in Oakland was a workingman's bookshop where all books were a dime. With or without David I never left that shop with less than fifty cents' worth of books—five, that means, my first find being a brilliant copy of Horace McCoy's *They Shoot Horses, Don't They?*—the famous novel about the marathon dances that had once been popular. Proletarian literature was just coming into vogue with scouts and collectors, and the McCoy book was a modest prize.

The dominant East Bay bookshop in those years was the Holmes Book Company in Oakland, a wonderful large bookshop with a big wraparound balcony devoted to fiction. That balcony, not to mention the Holmes Book Company in general, could always reward as much time as I could give it. I visited when I could; the one book I bought from them that I still have is Lady Anne Blunt's account of her travels in the Nejd, the cornerstone of what, many years later, became a two-thousand-volume collection of travel narratives by women.

I have a hard time separating those early trips with David Meltzer to the East Bay bookshops from later visits I made after I had become a dealer. Oakland and Berkeley were always worth scouting, particularly after Peter Howard got Serendipity going.

23

DURING MUCH OF my year as a Stegner fellow I did most of my writing in a three-dollar-a-night hotel on Geary Street. Not far away, on O'Fallon, was Mr. Dunlop's bookshop, its windows piled high with books. A few blocks away, on Turk Street, was a large store called McDonald's, then run by a grizzled bookman called Paisan, though not by me.

It was in McDonald's that I glimpsed the then most famous living book scout, I. R. (Ike) Brussel, who had "Last of the Great Scouts" printed on his quote cards. He was not the last, and opinions vary as to whether he was the greatest book scout, but I was glad to have glimpsed him, anyway. His son-in-law was a carpenter–book scout named Miles Caprilow, who once offered me the vanished poet Weldon Kees's copy of *Permit Me Voyage,* James Agee's first book. At $35 it was well beyond my means.

In San Francisco, as my Stegner year wound down, I worked a little on *Memories of the Old Tribe,* soon to be retitled *Leaving Cheyenne,* but otherwise did little writing. Often I was distracted by my neighbor's giant macaw, which was rarely quiet.

Meanwhile I was adjusting to a foggy new culture that I only half liked (the bookshops) and half hated (the chill, the fog, and the self-satisfied San Franciscans). Later I would discover that I much preferred Los Angeles, but after all, I was there only about nine months, and did my best to adapt.

At first I was merely startled by the broad cultural differences. If I asked for tea I got it hot, rather than iced, as was the universal custom in Texas. Hamburgers, in Texas, were flat like sandals and about as tasty; in San Francisco, they were round like softballs. Most of these differences were trivial. San Francisco hamburgers were actually better than Texas hamburgers.

What I really couldn't adapt to was the cloudiness and the fog. I grew up in the sun and I needed it, which is why I spend so much time in Tucson now.

24

In May, just as Jo, Putnam, and I were leaving San Francisco to return to Texas (Fort Worth), *Horseman, Pass By* was published, and the publication, so long waited for, was anticlimactic. There was a book—unfortunately I felt very little, but almost at once, it was sold to the movies and soon produced. The reason for the speedy route to production—which usually takes several years—was that Paul Newman wanted to star in it, and did. The movie was called *Hud,* and it did well.

I visited the set for most of one day, establishing a practice which I still mainly hold to. Unless you're the director or the DP (director of photography), one day is long enough to spend on any movie set.

The movie sale brought in $10,000, which we used to move back to San Francisco, a city Jo happened to love. A few months before we got off, our son, James, was born. The movie money had not yet arrived and there was a considerable hospital bill to pay, and the necessity of paying it led to my taking my first job in a bookstore—or at least, the warehouse of a bookstore.

A young man named Bill Gilliland was then running the famous Mc-Murray's Book Store, in Dallas. I soon became friends with Bill and his rangy wife, Anne, and am still friends with them.

The job Bill offered me involved cleaning out the McMurray's warehouse, on Industrial Avenue. My pay was ninety cents an hour, but I was at last working with books and I didn't complain.

The one book I remember from my summer in the warehouse was Edward Dahlberg's *Bottom Dogs,* which contained an introduction by D. H. Lawrence. This was heady stuff, but I refrained from stealing it and later acquired a copy by legitimate means.

25

WE HUSTLED YOUNG James out to San Francisco, where we were, for a month or two, thanks to Hollywood, people of leisure.

This didn't work as well as it should have, so, after a period of separation, we decided to try Austin, where about the best thing that happened is that I finally figured out how to make my second novel, *Leaving Cheyenne*, work. What made it work was that I gave each character a time of life of their own. Gid (the rancher) got youth, Molly (the woman) got middle age, and Johnny (the cowboy) got age. The story bears some resemblance to François Truffaut's *Jules et Jim*.

Once I hit on this division I wrote the draft that worked in about three weeks, most of it with James sitting on my lap.

Bookwise, Austin was significant because while there I met two book-men who became friends, Franklin Gilliam and Anthony Newnham. The shop they ran was the famous Brick Row Book Shop, surely the best bookshop in Texas at that time.

The Brick Row had a long history. It was founded in New Haven by a bookseller named E. Byrne Hackett, who later moved it to New York, where he became, for a time, a player in that city's then rich rare book trade, with the likes of the famous Dr. A. S. W. Rosenbach among his competitors.

Byrne Hackett, like many bookmen who should have known better, bought aggressively at the two sales of the songwriter Jerome Kern's expensive library. Jerome Kern had evidently concluded that stocks would make more money for him than books. The Crash, which came soon after his second sale, proved him wrong. Mr. Hackett ruefully told Franklin that it had taken him ten years to sell for $50 books he had paid $500 for in the Kern sale.

In any case Franklin bought the store in the fifties and moved it to Austin, a few blocks from the Harry Ransom Center at the University of Texas—the HRC was and still is a major acquirer of rare books and authors' archives.

Acquirers, particularly if they are institutional acquirers, need appraisers. The gentlemen of the Brick Row, who lived practically next door to the HRC, could have probably made a good living just appraising for that great holding.

Unfortunately, life is not that orderly—various things, including, particularly, romance, in the lives of both Franklin and Anthony led them seriously astray.

Franklin Gilliam, originally from Texas (Cuero), was born out of his place and his age; he was meant to sit in his club, read *The Times* of London, occasionally look out the window and say "harrumph!" He was especially fond of trains. With his teammate, Anthony, he was, for a time, able to arrange long, cozy buying trips, always by train, across America, Canada, and the British Isles.

Anthony Newnham, by contrast, was a Byronic Englishman who, in the fullness of time, married something like nine women; these unions produced I don't know how many children. With the onset of pregnancy Anthony's interest in a given wife was likely to go into sharp decline. In his young manhood he had worked for Bertram Rota, a pioneer in the sale of modern first editions. Bertram Rota Ltd still exists, but Anthony Newnham is long gone. Anthony knew nineteenth-century English books and autographs as well as any dealer I've known. For a time he had his own bookshop on the Isle of Wight, but he allowed Franklin to move him to Austin, where he produced a string of excellent catalogues with a heavy emphasis on the nineteenth century. Anthony was a very disciplined man, and energetic to an extreme, whereas his partner, Franklin, liked to wander around in his bathrobe drinking tea all morning, after which he would get dressed and amble off to a leisurely lunch; then he might catalogue a few books for his long a-building Southern catalogue, have a martini, and proceed to a long dinner, during which, well into the second or third bottle of wine, he would usually nod off.

Even when his formidable mother, Maggie, was brought in to prod Franklin into working a little harder, Franklin clung to his habits and was often still in his bathrobe as luncheon approached.

One of my peculiarities as a book scout was that I soon developed an uncanny ability to find books inscribed by Franklin Gilliam to various former girlfriends, all of whom seemed to have sold them the next day. The first time this happened was at the Lost Generation bookshop, then in McLean, Virginia, where I bought three Eragny Press books, all inscribed by Franklin to an unknown female. The Eragny Press was founded by the painter Lucien Pissarro—over time it produced a few distinctive books and a certain number of duds.

By the time I made this discovery the Brick Row had moved to San Francisco, where Franklin and his wife, Jacqueline, and her daughter Vivian were living in some elegance.

When I called Franklin to ask if he had ever inscribed any Eragny Press books to anyone there was dead silence on the line. Then Franklin began to expostulate in an unhappy fashion.

The three Eragny Press books turned out to be only the tip of the iceberg. At some point Jacqueline became Franklin's ex-wife, and time came when she needed money. She had good books, about two hundred of which we bought. Of the two hundred, more than half had lavish inscriptions in Franklin's hand; a few of these inscriptions were in French, and a handful were mildly racy. The inscriptions seemed to suggest that the books were gifts, but somehow I doubt it. Franklin loved baseball and, once moved to the West Coast, became a loyal Giants fan, whose play he watched at Candlestick Park from the depths of an immense parka, only his binoculars extruding.

Once it fell to my lot to raise a litter of basset puppies, belonging to the family of my partner, Marcia Carter. One of them bore such an uncanny resemblance to Franklin Gilliam that we named him Franklin.

As the dog Franklin aged, his resemblance to the man Franklin did not diminish. From time to time the two would cross paths in one bookshop or another, neither suspecting that they shared a name.

Those in the know were paralyzed with embarrassment when the two Franklins turned up at the same time in the same store. The person who inadvertently revealed the name sharing was the mild Bill Matheson, then head of rare books at the Library of Congress. "Who would have thought that dog would grow up to be so ugly?" he said, in the presence of Franklin Gilliam. For a time there was a *froideur,* but it passed, and after a time Franklin Gilliam seemed to become mildly fond of his namesake.

The little ripple over the dog was nothing compared to the rift (with Jacqueline, not us) over the inscriptions. Jacqueline had sold us very nice books, which, naturally, we put right on the shelves of Booked Up, in Georgetown.

Franklin, in those days, was a rather languid book buyer. He visited us twice without picking up a single book. He sat, chatted, drank beer, didn't scout. Marcia and I debated erasing the inscriptions, but that would have meant a lot of erasing. In the end we left them in place, and one day, sure enough, Franklin wandered over to a shelf, idly picked up a book, and looked inside. No man ever went scarlet quicker—the shock was so great that for a time he had to sit down.

Though we had done nothing wrong, I can't remember that he was ever in Booked Up again, though that was probably because of ill health rather than pique. Franklin had begun to shuffle.

To mollify him we gave him an album that had come with our purchase from Jacqueline. It was a scrapbook or commonplace book, in a lovely morocco binding, and had been acquired many years earlier by Byrne Hackett at the Kern sale. It was thought then that there might be a verse or two in Shelley's hand, but this proved not to be the case—not, at least, according to Arthur Freeman, the learned American who comprised part of the brain trust of the great English firm of Quaritch for many years.

Anthony Newnham tended mainly to marry against type. His first wife, I am told, was a proper English housewife—thus, in America, he usually went for wild, drug-taking motorcycle girls. One of his wives, Janie Butterfield, now deceased, was a good friend of mine; she had also been close to the Texas novelist William Brammer.

Anthony's method, subconscious as it may have been, was to marry wild American girls and turn them into proper English housewives—if they submitted to this change he rapidly lost interest. He was a very attractive man, even though, for a time, he had no front teeth, these having been knocked out by a cricket ball when he was nine. He lost his bridge and, for some years, didn't bother to replace it.

Besides being a very good bookman, Anthony was also a master carpenter, who, once he gave up on book selling in Texas, began a second career as a builder of houses for rock stars. I believe he built one for Leon Russell, in Oklahoma, and he later worked on one at Malibu.

All along he kept on marrying and siring children he could not support. Finally he went back to England, a child-support fugitive.

Once he left these shores I never saw him again. He married once more and tried to get on with Quaritch—I heard that he was judged to be too senior. Certainly he knew nineteenth-century English books as well as anyone.

Anthony moved to Edinburgh and continued, for a time, to issue his distinctive, oblong catalogues, oblong being his favorite format since his days on the Isle of Wight.

He fell dead, I'm told, while lifting a wineglass to his lips—an ideal exit, all things considered.

26

THE BRICK ROW Book Shop, under Franklin Gilliam and Anthony Newnham, flourished in a day when university librarians were eager to have booksellers fill out their holdings in certain agreed-upon areas. Franklin and Anthony applied themselves to what might loosely be called the Edwardian period, which, in their case, meant 1885 to 1915, more or less. The period suited Franklin's taste, whereas lots of periods suited Anthony's taste. When I knew him he was working hard on a bibliography of Evelyn Waugh, doomed to be uncompleted.

The two of them would take a train to some big university—possibly in Canada, possibly the States. There they would spend some days with the card catalogue (none of *those* left) and would eventually come up with a list of several thousand books they would supply if they could find them.

Usually they had a limit they could charge on the open quotation system. Armed with their lists they would chug down to Acres of Books, in Cincinnati, a shop that once had nearly a quarter of a million volumes of fiction, alphabetized. Most of the books were priced fifty cents—this was long ago. In Austin these fifty-cent books would become fifteen-dollar books when sent back to the university, which then purchased them.

It was a living—or at least a good start on one.

Franklin eventually moved the Brick Row to San Francisco, where it exists today, admirably run by John Crichton.

It's a movable entity, with a long history, as such things go.

27

I HAVE LONG been fascinated by the popularity of pulp fiction, and keep a small selection of pulp magazines, mainly from the thirties. Also, my interest extends backward, into the pulp fiction of the nineteenth century, mainly in its most popular form, the penny dreadful.

It was from the Brick Row that I bought my first penny dreadful, the penny parts bound in a nice calf binding. Penny dreadfuls were then common enough on the antiquarian market. I paid $45 for my first one, and in time acquired seven or eight, including the famous *Sweeney Todd, the Demon Barber of Fleet Street,* now a film starring Johnny Depp.

I eventually sold the penny dreadfuls but kept my small collection of twentieth-century American pulps. I'm hanging on to them against the day when I might want to write something Legmanesque about violence in American popular culture.

In writing so briefly about book scouting in the Bay Area, I realize I've failed to remember a few notable eccentrics then in the booktrade there.

My favorite was a small Jewish man whose name I have forgotten. He operated in one room with very high shelves in a shop not far from the *San Francisco Chronicle.* This dealer insisted that his customers look at his books through binoculars: he wasn't particularly unfriendly—it's just that he only had one room, shelved very high. He let me peer through the binoculars as long as I wanted to—I never saw another customer in the store.

On my very first visit to that shop I was rewarded by the discovery of a book that was very salable down the 101 in Hollywood: Mrs. D. W. Griffith's *My Life in Movies*. Larry Edmunds, the famous movie bookshop on Hollywood Boulevard, with which I had had some dealings and was to have more, put a nippy price on Mrs. Griffith's book: $25, as I remember. My first copy cost $1. I sold it to Larry Edmunds for $10 and they were glad to get it. On my next visit to the high-shelved shop I found another copy, also priced $1. Eventually I bought eight copies, although by then Milt Luboviski, who owned and operated Larry Edmunds with his wife, Git, and others, came to the odd conclusion that the copies I sent them were piracies and stopped buying, even though I lowered the asking price to $5. It seemed to me clear enough that I happened onto a remainder, not a piracy. Later I bought a lovely, inscribed copy of Mrs. Griffith's book in Mexico City, and I still have it. I don't know how many copies the little man with the binoculars had because the next time I went to his shop the door was locked, and so far as I know, the bookman never came back.

28

I COULD RARELY get David Meltzer to venture down the peninsula with me. He was mainly an East Bay scout; he had a family to support and the pickings were just richer across the Bay Bridge.

Nonetheless I liked to go south, because if I went far enough south, to Los Gatos or San Jose, I could emerge from under what is now called the marine layer—that is, fog and gloom—and see some sun, which I needed more than I needed the few books I might come home with. One of my favorite bookshops in that direction was in San Carlos; its owners kept a big parrot that always squawked at me when I turned into the fiction aisle.

San Jose, in 1960, was a village compared to what it is now, but it boasted three or four shops whose wares were modestly priced. It was in San Jose that I bought my only really pristine copy of Wright Morris's *The Home Place,* a book fairly hard to locate, even then.

My days have always been, to one degree or another, book filled, but never more so than in my first year in San Francisco: there were more antiquarian book shops there than I could possibly cover, but I did my best and hugely enjoyed the hunt.

Today the only book in my twenty-eight thousand volumes to survive from that year is a little book in the New Directions New Classics series: Ezra Pound's *ABC of Reading,* a book I still reread every five years or so.

I bought it from the Discovery Bookstore, rather late at night.

29

Now on to the David family, in particular Grace David and her son, Dorman, though her daughter, Diane, and her onetime (no, two-time) husband, Henry David, also play a part in the story, which took place in Houston in the early and mid-sixties.

Grace David, now in her mid-nineties and still my friend, came from a ranching family near Mason, Texas, which is in the hill country west of Austin and San Antonio.

It is well known that the great art collectors Jean and Dominique de Menil commissioned the first Philip Johnson house to be built in Houston; it's less well known that Grace David commissioned the second. (Or so I understand; much about the Davids belongs to legend rather than to fact. And Philip Johnson's reputation is no longer what it then was.)

C. Dorman David, Grace's son, was, for the first twenty-some years of his life, dyslexic. This condition was finally correctly diagnosed and cured. Dorman—once he could read books—developed a desire to trade in them. He was not without means, either. His father, Henry David, arranged for his children to receive some trust money while he himself was still very much alive. Dorman's share was rumored to be a million and a half—Diane's, I assume, was the same.

With this bankroll Dorman proposed to set up as a rare book man. In the early sixties a million and a half would certainly take you some distance toward building a stock of rare books—but not if one did it the way Dorman did it.

First, he decided that he needed to apprentice himself to a master bookseller, and the bookman he chose was Warren Howell of San Francisco, who, at the time, had the most imposing book room of any dealer on the West Coast. More important, he had the stock to fill it.

Legend has it that when Dorman David went up Post Street to ask Warren Howell for a job, he kept a cab waiting at the curb. That legend somehow followed Dorman through his brief career as a bookseller.

Warren Howell was usually kind to young dealers, and perhaps not so kind to his peers. Maybe he took a liking to this bumptious young Texan, or perhaps he sensed early that there might be money to be made, somewhere down the line. Anyway, he hired Dorman, but soon let him go; the prevailing theory on Dorman's brief stay with Howell was that he was simply buying everything good that came in in the Texana line, books for which Warren Howell may have had other, steadier customers—customers whose displeasure he risked if he kept on letting Dorman buy so much.

Whatever the truth of that, Dorman went home and busied himself by designing a beautiful bookshop, which he did. The main room was a great cube, with shelves going way up to the ceiling. There was a humidor room, in which Dorman planned to sell rare tobaccos. For a safe he had the boll of a Louisiana gum tree: striking, and also fireproof. The house was on San Felipe, not far from the de Menils and other grandees. At some point a Japanese houseboy enjoyed a brief tenure. His job was to serve sherry, or sake, or whatever.

With his building in hand, all Dorman needed was a stock. Undaunted, but with much of his million and a half gone, Dorman set off on a tour of the major dealers in Texana and Americana generally. He went to the Eberstadts, then the deans of the Americanists. He went to Lathrop Harper. He went east and he went west, buying choice items, but at stiff prices. In general the major dealers were intrigued with Dorman, but not so intrigued that they forgot how to work the cash register. Here was a young man who made selling fun.

By the time Dorman opened he had a fine if pricey stock of Western books, as well as something like a quarter of the items mentioned in Thomas Streeter's *Bibliography of Texas,* or at least that was Franklin Gilliam's estimate.

Attached to the bookshop was a gallery where Dorman proposed to sell Western landscapes, some of which he had, and none of which were acquired cheaply (though some, probably, were consigned).

It eventually fell to Dorman's sister, Diane, to dispose of much of the Western art.

There was a grand opening, which I did not attend. Instead I wandered in a few days later and bought a signed, limited copy of Dr. Rosenbach's *Early American Children's Books,* for which I paid a pittance.

Dorman chased me down and asked for it back—it was supposed to be part of his reference library, though, as far as I could see, there was no reference library. I reluctantly yielded it up, taking some Tarzan first editions in exchange. The Tarzans looked pretty silly in that grand room.

This was the first of a number of puzzling, ambiguous trades I made with Dorman David, in which I always seemed to come out the winner. In one trade I came away with a Mercedes coupé, a vehicle far beyond my skills. In another I got an excellent pool table, which I still have.

Dorman, like Grace, seemed to simply attract good things: it might be a Purdey shotgun today, or a Rolls-Royce tomorrow. Not only did he attract them, he was always willing to trade; but he seemed to come out on the losing end in most of these trades. They can rarely have been good for his business, which, after all, was in rare books. At one juncture he acquired a cannon collection, an asset not easily moved. Dealers began to fly into Houston in droves just a little less heavy than the droves of passenger pigeons must have been. One, I hear, traded a modestly valuable

Huxley manuscript and some kind of a guitar for a fine copy of *Three Stories and Ten Poems,* Ernest Hemingway's first book. (This, of course, could be legend.)

I am not sure exactly how long Dorman managed to hang on, but it was not long. Then he flamed out. A hasty selection of his rarest books went to the auction rooms. The major dealers got back their treasures for modest sums and, as good dealers will, proceeded to sell them again.

Dorman fled to Mexico.

The auction had not yielded enough: the threat of bankruptcy loomed.

And then in strode Grace, a woman of indomitable spirit, who flatly refused to have her son be a bankrupt. She took over and hired her friend Deena, who had once been a librarian, somewhere, I think. The two of them took over, determined to run this bookshop, and by gosh and by golly, they did.

Soon they got a call from the Yount family in Beaumont: the Younts had been partially responsible for bringing in the Spindletop oilfield, and thus naturally had a mansion containing a huge for-show library—there were something like nineteen sets of de Maupassant alone.

The Yount books in their thousands were brought to Houston and piled in heaps in the great room of the Bookman. I wandered in one day, just scouting, and there were Grace and Deena, buried beneath piles of books they knew absolutely nothing about. Grace was graphic and tactile: print was not her thing. What I saw were two nice ladies who had no idea how to proceed. The library they had acquired, though vast, was nearly worthless.

I suggested that I help them, was hired on the spot, and began one of the best friendships of my life, with Grace David, who faced many discouragements with a powerful spirit. I worked for her for two and a half years, along the way acquiring for the Bookman the general stock of the Larry Edmunds bookshop—I'm not sure Git Luboviski has ever forgiven me for that cultural rape. But that stock, eclectic and sophisticated, helped make up a little for the nineteen sets of de Maupassant.

Grace was married at the time to Henry David; as a young man in the oilfields Henry had developed a superior kind of drilling mud and became very rich. At some point before I entered the story, Henry sold his company for many millions of dollars, after which he had nothing to do but drink, play golf, and watch his wife and children spend his money on things that were, to him, meaningless: art, pots, tropical fish, sculpture, woodcraft, telephones. (Grace never liked being more than a step from a telephone; at one point the Bookman had nineteen.)

Henry sober was a nice man; Henry drunk was to be avoided, as Grace was well aware. She kept a bicycle by her bed, in case she needed to flee; she also saw to it that there were about a dozen doors between her bedroom and Henry's—once, at least, she locked herself out of all twelve.

She loved architecture, and was always buying and selling houses, some of which she then rebought. She, Dorman, and Diane were constantly trading with one another: it might be a Stuart table, it might be a totem pole, but it was not likely to be books.

30

I was very happy running the Bookman. There was an element of craziness about it, but that can be said of many bookshops. The *objets* Grace traded for were always attractive, whether a Greek cheese board or Hungarian shepherd's crook. I still wish I'd bought that shepherd's crook.

As a commercial venture the Bookman was hopeless from the first. At one point Grace had a penthouse built onto the property—the penthouse contained a wall-sized aquarium, containing hundreds of lovely, mysterious fish. What it cost to maintain I never knew.

Needless to say there were ruckuses with Henry, who watched millions of dollars flowing away, to purchase items he had no interest in. Some days he might come home from the golf course to find that Grace had made a unilateral decision to separate from him. In these cases she simply called the movers; there was a small company that made a sufficient career just out of moving the Davids. They would come get Henry's stuff and haul it out to a house he kept on the golf course. The move would be completed between nine and five. I came to have great affection for the gentlemen of this moving company. They knew just how to handle each of the hundreds of *objets* the Davids owned. They had some trouble with the cannon collection, but otherwise were adequate to the profusion the Davids threw at them. Whatever it happened to be, they were well aware that pretty soon they would be moving it again.

When she was feeling secure about money Grace was very generous with her children, and with me. She sent me on two buying trips to the East Coast, and one to the West Coast. In New York I was just in time to visit the great Seven Gables Bookshop before it closed, and to meet the two learned veterans who ran it: Michael Papantonio and John S. Van E. Kohn. I visited the Scribner Rare Book Shop and scuttled downtown to rummage in the deteriorating Dauber & Pine.

In Hollywood, where I was soon to be employed as a screenwriter, I found that on Hollywood Boulevard, at least, bookshops stayed open very late, as they had in San Francisco. The brothers Lou and Ben Weinstein had moved up from Compton and gone full-out as booksellers. They called themselves the Heritage Book Shop and are just now closing, after forty-four years.

One reason I took some not very promising screenwriting jobs was so that, once freed from story conferences, I could hustle up to Hollywood Boulevard and buy books.

Grace paid me well and paid me happily. The Bookman slowly acquired a respectable stock, and even issued a respectable sequence of catalogues.

Kind and gracious as Grace always was to me, it was not always thus with her children—especially Dorman.

Grace would be seized with fits of financial paranoia—if it *was* paranoia. Henry must often have been tempted to close the whole show down. What could he make of a wife who could spend hundreds of thousands of dollars a year on fish?

When the attacks of insecurity came on her, Dorman was always the person Grace landed on first.

Dorman night be sitting in his apartment staring at two traffic tickets he didn't have the money to pay, when Grace would call and demand the $200,000 he owed her, now!

One of these fits of financial panic occurred while I was in New York on a buying trip. Grace called Dorman and told him to get over there with the money, quick!

One reason to go, for Dorman, was that, while he might not have ten bucks in his pocket, he always had *stuff*: Chinese coins or Mayan artifacts—the Mayan pieces were mostly fakes, but no one knew that at the time, except, of course, the faker. Dorman was still attracting every trader in the region: one day he bought something like nineteen hundred lithograph stones, to do what with no one can say.

This time, with me out of town, Dorman wandered over to his mother's with some excellent Texana—letters from Sam Houston, Stephen F. Austin, and the like, most of them addressed to the commandant of the port of Galveston. These documents were of the first importance, dealing, as they did, with the Texans' effort to free themselves from Mexico.

Grace herself wouldn't have known a Stephen F. Austin letter from a possum, but she did know that the documents must be pretty valuable because Dorman had taken them to Yale and offered them to Archibald Hanna, the librarian most likely to purchase high-end Texana.

Archibald Hanna turned them down, very possibly because he knew where they ought to be.

I had working for us at the Bookman then a just-graduated student named Mike Evans, who had returned from Cambridge, England, where he had been exchanged in some sort of advanced-swap program for Michael Pakenham, Lady Antonia Fraser's younger brother. Mike, now forty years on, teaches school in rural Virginia, but he has remained book alert and still comes down from time to time to help us out in the summers.

I have always believed in having as many reference books as possible, although, of course, in the Age of Google, they are not as vital as they were in 1966. We had reference books that enabled Mike, in a matter of minutes, to determine that the pile of documents Dorman was prepared to give his mother as collateral were indeed very valuable. There was just one catch: according to the reference books the whole lot belonged in the Rosenberg Library in Galveston.

Dorman David, it must be admitted, was an impulsive man. If Charlton

Heston walked up to him with a piece of rock with ten commandments scratched on it, Dorman would not be the one to question their authenticity very long. He would buy the rock and figure it out later.

I don't pretend to know the truth about those Galveston documents. I don't know how they made their way from the Rosenberg Library to the great room at the Bookman. But I did know that we had stumbled into a huge crisis. We had a great number of documents on our hands that were very probably stolen.

Obviously, we could *not* sell them.

Grace was horrified, no doubt envisioning Henry's wrath when he discovered that another $200,000 had flown out the door.

It was at this juncture that I left the Bookman. I loved Grace and still do, but we simply could not sell those documents. At my insistence they were put in a safe-deposit box—about ten years passed before the matter was concluded, to the extent that it could be said to be concluded. I'm not sure it was ever really settled. Dorman had some minor trouble with the law—once I heard that some of the documents had been given to the University of Houston as part of a plea bargain. A few may have trickled up to the Austin bookseller Johnny Jenkins, who, later still, was found shot to death in a river near Bastrop, Texas. Johnny had another identity, as a high-stakes poker player in Las Vegas, where he was known as Austin Squatty. Whether his death was suicide or murder I don't know, though someone must.

Grace David, having failed to evade Henry while he was in a wrathful state—a near-fatal mistake—sensibly closed the Bookman and moved to London, then Switzerland, then Santa Barbara. Before Grace left, Mike Evans ran the Bookman for a while—even Anthony Newnham took off from his celebrity carpentry for a while, to run the shop. He issued one of his trademark oblong catalogues, this one devoted to Mark Twain; but no amount of diligence on the part of any bookseller could compensate for the vortexlike downward spiral of the Davids as they were then.

I am very glad that Grace survived Henry—it was, for a while, a near thing. She even oversaw the building of another great house, before she left Houston. The Bookman is now not a bookshop.

The architects, the painters, the artists, the wood-carvers, the pot makers, and the weavers all miss Grace David—who helped them all out from time to time. I suspect the gentlemen of the little moving company miss her too . . . as I do.

31

ONCE I LEFT the Bookman I continued to scout as much as possible, sometimes ranging as far afield as Austin and San Antonio. In the latter city I particularly enjoyed Norman Brock's vast store. Poor broke Brock, they called Norman, who was incapable of refusing any offering, whether it was a book or a merry-go-round.

Perhaps my greatest scouting disappointment occurred at Brock's. One day, as I was descending to the basement, which Norman eventually filled to the very brim, I saw what looked to be a perfect copy of Nathanael West's *A Cool Million,* a few steps down, under a few novels.

I had never seen the book before, and was very excited, only to discover, when I pulled it out, that rats had chewed off the back cover. I remember the shock of disappointment to this day.

When home in Archer City, I had to make do, scoutingwise, with a good paperback exchange on Monroe Street in Wichita Falls. Evidently a local minister, perhaps too sensitive for his environment, decided he didn't want to be local anymore. He sold his library to the paperback exchange, although his books were hardback. The mistress of the shop priced each of them at fifty cents. I got a nice copy of James Baldwin's *Go Tell It on the Mountain,* and sold it to Newton Taylor, a San Francisco bookseller who, as far as I can discover, is active no more.

32

A few years after Booked Up opened in Georgetown, Washington, D.C., our friend Allan Stypeck bought a small bookshop called Second Story Books, on Connecticut Avenue. Allan flourished, and over time, Second Story Books migrated into several locations, from Baltimore to Georgetown.

In Georgetown they occupied a building that had once housed the Savile Book Shop, which sold new books. Second Story in Georgetown was only a few blocks from Booked Up, and I was in it often. It was from the Georgetown Second Story that I picked up a really rare book and immediately underpriced it.

Then, a few hours later, I sold it to a newcomer to the rare book trade, W. Hallam Webber, previously a coin dealer. Hallam likes to think that he is the model for Cadillac Jack in my novel of that name, but I picked that name off a D.C. street corner where two pimps were talking about a third pimp who had just cruised by in a Cadillac.

It is certainly true that Hallam and Jack share certain trading instincts.

The book I got at Second Story that day was the Marquis de Sade's *Justine,* the first edition of which is an easily acquired book. But this *wasn't* the first edition. It contained a few erotic engravings, meant to be dirty but not likely to raise much heat today. The book was priced $350—with my dealer's discount I got it for $280.

Our neighbor Bill Hale, also a book dealer, was with me when I made the purchase. I offered to bet him that I could sell the book that afternoon to Hallam Webber for $750.

Bill Hale didn't bet, but I did handily sell the book to Hal Webber that afternoon for $750.

A profit of nearly $500 was not to be sneezed at, in those days or these days either.

Hallam Webber then flung himself into a frenzy of research that took several months to complete. When he finally resurfaced Hallam announced that the book we had sold him was the extremely rare *second* edition of *Justine*—extremely rare because the French censors had destroyed almost the whole edition. The copy had belonged in turn to two famous collectors, Prince Galitzin (of Russia) and a man we now think to be Frederick Hankey, a creepy Parisian collector of erotica well described by G. Legman in *The Horn Book*.

The book contained Hankey's small circular photographic bookplate, a thing in itself pretty rare.

The moral is the same old moral most booksellers agree on: you can't know everything.

Hal Webber eventually sold the book for—I believe—$8,000.

33

SOMETIME IN THE mid-seventies I began to view myself as essentially a bookseller—or maybe just a book scout. The hunt for books was what absorbed me most. Writing was my vocation, but I had written a lot, and it was no longer exactly a passion.

While in San Francisco, I often visited the Argonaut Book Shop, on Sutter Street, an excellent shop run by Robert Haines (and now run by his children). Robert Haines sold a little bit of everything but his heart was mainly in Americana.

One day out of the blue he wrote me (I was then at Rice) and offered me five excellent author collections of modern literature for a little over $100 a collection: Hemingway, Faulkner, Sinclair Lewis, Edwin Arlington Robinson, and Steinbeck.

To say that I was surprised would be an understatement—I didn't really know Robert Haines that well. I think he probably needed space and expected to do well enough from the Americana in his purchase that he could afford to jettison the literature.

I at once paid the Argonaut $600 and sold the collections to Rice for $1,000. To gild the lily a bit I called myself Dust Bowl Books and issued a leaflet, which I mimeographed on the English Department copier. That leaflet is now more rare than any of the books it describes.

The collection did not contain the three pricey first books: *Three Stories and Ten Poems* (Hemingway), *The Marble Faun* (Faulkner), and *Hike and the Aeroplane* (Lewis), but all the other books were there, and they were there in exceptional condition: essentially unread and as new. We have sold many of the books that were in that collection several times, but never in the condition the Argonaut books were in. I remember them with amazement, and wonder how Robert Haines settled on me to sell them to.

Something startling has occurred in the world of high-end dust wrappers. The much-collected classic *Anne of Green Gables,* by L. M. Montgomery, has been for long thought to have been issued without dust wrapper; but in book collecting and bibliography few certainties remain unchallenged. In the case of *Anne of Green Gables,* a book scout has recently turned up what appears to be a (so far) unique copy of the first edition dust wrapper for that much-collected book.

The only awkwardness about this much-desired dust wrapper is that it comes unattached to a book. At least one collector wants to "marry" the dust wrapper to his first issue of the book. If he succeeds, the price for the dust wrapper will likely be in six figures. Holy cow!

34

THE REASON I made my gifted antique scout Cadillac Jack an antique scout instead of a book scout is that I know how hard it is to get the "common reader," if such creatures still exist, interested in the arcane detail that is involved in antiquarian book scouting.

Some people, of course, are frankly more attached to their possessions than they are to people, but that doesn't take you very far if you're trying to deal with them in fiction.

Here I am, thirty-four chapters into a book that I hope will interest the general or common reader—and yet why should these readers be interested in the fact that in 1958 or so I paid Ted Brown $7.50 for a nice copy of *The Anatomy of Melancholy*? How many are going to care that I visited the great Seven Gables Bookshop, or dealt with the wily L.A. dealer Max Hunley, whose little store at the corner of Rodeo Drive and Little Santa Monica in Beverly Hills is now a yogurt shop? Why should they even care that there exists a possibly unique copy of the dust wrapper of *Anne of Green Gables*?

A fair answer would be that few readers are engaged by this kind of stuff, unless the writer can somehow tap deeper sentiments. A general reader named Helen Hanff tapped these sentiments in *84 Charing Cross Road*, a book about her relations, all epistolary, with the English bookman Frank Doel, who worked for a bookshop called Marks & Co., at the address that gave Ms. Hanff her title. Frank Doel was only doing what any professional bookman would do, but Ms. Hanff hit the nerve anyway.

There have been few best sellers about book selling, and only a relatively few fictions that make use of the secondhand bookshop as a setting. There's a bookshop in Raymond Chandler's *The Big Sleep*, and it is also in the movie. *Unfaithful*, the recent Richard Gere/Diane Lane movie, features Richard Gere as a bookseller. Earlier on there were Arnold Bennett's *Riceyman Steps* and Christopher Morley's *The Haunted Bookshop;* more recently, the bibliomysteries of John Dunning, as well as those of Marianne MacDonald.

The bibliomystery is now, it seems, a collecting field. Somehow or other, in the eighties, Booked Up actually owned what was said to be the first bibliomystery, a mid-nineteenth-century book called *Scrope.* Better than the book itself was the gentleman who bought our one copy: Sarkis Shmavonian, whose appearance on the American book scene has been colorful. We saw him only the once.

35

AFTER THE BOOKMAN ceased to be my principal book place, Houston began to lose its appeal for me. I liked book selling a lot, more than I liked teaching, even though I had the ideal teaching job at the ideal school.

Teaching simply ceased to engage me, whereas rare book dealing interested me more and more. In a way I was getting bored not merely with Rice but with book selling in Texas generally. Herbert Fletcher moved to Salado; Joe Petty, with his rich holdings of Romain Rolland, moved to Victoria; and the Brick Row moved to San Francisco.

In Dallas Sawnie Aldredge died and the Harpers were near to giving up. In Austin there was Johnny Jenkins, with whom I never had much rapport, though we did a deal from time to time.

(There's a book called *Texfake*, written by the former bookseller W. Thomas Taylor, with an introduction by me, in which there are descriptions of both Dorman David and John H. Jenkins III.)

In San Francisco I had enjoyed a modicum of literary society, whereas in Texas I had little or none.

In San Francisco I had also acquired my first and most beloved agent, Dorothea Oppenheimer, a beautiful and volatile European woman who had grown up very rich in a castle on the Rhine—or was it the Danube? She had gone to school with the future duke of Edinburgh, saw the Nazis take her family's money, fled to New York, worked for *The New Yorker*, charmed and seduced many, and came to San Francisco for reasons I do not know. She lived on Vallejo Street, in Pacific Heights; at some point she invited me to the first cocktail party I ever went to. We had our ups and downs, but Dorothea remained my agent until her death more than thirty years later, though, in her last, sad days—she died of pancreatic cancer—Irving Paul Lazar, "Swifty" as he came to be known, did a good bit of the legwork for her.

Dorothea could be wonderful and also could be maddening: of all the young writers she helped out, only I and, I believe, Ernest Gaines remained clients to the end.

I only found out how old Dorothea was—seventy-six—the last time I saw her, by which time she had been reduced to a one-room studio apartment on York Avenue, a long way from that castle on the Danube, or the Rhine.

36

THE NEXT BIG event in my life with books was the disposal at auction of the stock of the long-dominant D.C. book-selling firm of Lowdermilks, on F Street in downtown Washington.

This auction occurred in the early months of 1970. I was working on the script of *The Last Picture Show* at the time and had to fly the red-eye in order not to miss the first day of the sale. Marcia Carter, my elegant, long-time book-selling partner, and I had decided we wanted to run a bookshop together, and the quicker the better, and the auction of Lowdermilks seemed a good place to start accumulating a stock.

As it turned out, the auction was very worth the red-eye, for the dispersal of Lowdermilks's huge stock was the real beginning of Booked Up, the bookshop Marcia and I ran together for some thirty-six years. We were thirty-two years in Georgetown before rising rents forced us to take the stock to Texas, where it still abides.

37

THE 1970S—DECADE OF the Lowdermilks sale—was part of the sad era that saw the closing of downtown urban bookshops in many American cities. The great dinosaurs began to disappear: Leary's in Philadelphia, Lowdermilks in Washington, Goodspeed's on Milk Street in Boston, Dauber & Pine and various others in New York City, Acres of Books in Cincinnati, and a little later, the Holmes Book Company in Oakland. These were venerable bookshops all, and those who loved them miss them still.

What these closings revealed was no secret to anyone in the trade: secondhand books can't keep up with downtown real estate values, unless a shop is very well established and manages to become a kind of regional institution—Powell's in Portland, Oregon; the Strand in New York City; and the Tattered Cover (new books) in Denver. These stores survive because many, many people take sustenance from them.

A good many people take sustenance from our store, Booked Up, also, although it's located in a town fully two hours from the nearest international airport (Dallas/Fort Worth).

We took Booked Up to Archer City because the real estate there was cheap enough to allow us to house our three-hundred-thousand-volume stock, which we could not afford to do in any sizable city. After all, in relatively cheap Fort Worth, Barber's Book Store, admirably run at the time I bought it, survived seventy years and then ceased to survive. Or almost. I hear the last owner, Bryan Perkins, is still selling books somewhere nearby—entrance through a coffee shop.

Many once-great stores—I think of Shorey's in Seattle and the West Coast Acres of Books in Long Beach (soon to cease to be, its owner told me recently)—exist as mere shadows of their former selves.

38

LOWDERMILKS—TO GET BACK to the story—was auctioned by the venerable Philadelphia firm of Freeman's.

As a book buyer I had visited Lowdermilks several times, but my visits were brief and hardly scratched the surface of their massive stock, which occupied three floors of a large old building downtown. The third floor had not been visited (except by favored customers) for about ten years, or at least that was the legend. This floor contained a huge accumulation of nineteenth-century books.

Since I had been in Hollywood during the viewing period, Marcia and I went into the auction flying blind.

Freeman's had the task of disposing some half million volumes in a short amount of time. This was not the famous John Marion of Sotheby's trying to coax one more million out of a rich bidder for a fine Cézanne. Getting these half million books sold required pace, not finesse. The cataloguing was of the simplest. A typical entry might read "six hundred volumes literature" or "four hundred volumes biography."

We two, the embryonic Booked Up, concentrated on these large lots, bidding about a quarter a book. To our astonishment we were often successful, ending up with about fifteen hundred books, all of them gleaned from the mysterious, dusty third floor.

At this time, because of all the screenwriting I was doing, my acquaintances in the trade were mostly West Coast booksellers: the Canterbury

99

Bookshop on Melrose, the Heritage, still on Hollywood Boulevard, and the glamorous Peggy Christian and others.

The Lowdermilks auction, of course, was held on the East Coast, and Freeman's salesrooms soon filled up with Eastern dealers, few of whom I knew. Johnny Jenkins was the only Texas dealer I spotted; he turned out to be the biggest buyer of the sale, sinking a good deal of money into government documents, of which Lowdermilks had a great many. He was so busy bidding that I don't think we ever spoke. There were only two dealers I remember distinctly, one being Clarence Wolf, known as the "wolf cub," because his uncle was the famous bookman-librarian-biographer Edwin Wolf.

Clarence Wolf bought so much at the Lowdermilks sale that he had to leave some of it—he ceded several rows of biography to us, or anyone else that wanted to tote it away.

One of the purposes of this narrative, as I've indicated, is to raise ghosts—often long-absent ghosts. One such, at the Lowdermilks sale, was the slightly mysterious dealer Jeff Rund, who dealt in high-end erotica. At the Lowdermilks sale I remember him mainly because he bought the one lot we coveted most: several issues of the famous literary magazine *The Little Review,* all of them heaped on a shelf on the third floor. *The Little Review* was perhaps the most celebrated of all American little magazines. Founded by Margaret Anderson in Chicago, it went on to flourish in Paris, edited then by Margaret Anderson and Jane Heap. Probably its most daring act was to publish several installments of James Joyce's *Ulysses.*

In all my years of book dealing I've had only a few issues of *The Little Review.* What happened to Jeff Rund I don't know—his is not now a name on many booksellers' lips. Despite his victory at that sale, if he's still alive, I wish him well.

39

FOR MUCH OF their long life in the capital city, Lowdermilks did some publishing too. Now and then during the sale, on quick forays to the third floor, we ran across piles of their remainders. Whether Lowdermilks ever published out-and-out erotica I don't know, but they did publish a book that gets marketed as erotica even to this day: *Scatological Rites of All Nations,* by John Gregory Bourke, the colorful pioneer ethnologist who for years was an aide-de-camp for the sometimes cranky General George Crook. Bourke seemed to deal better than most with Crook's dark moods.

The Indians called Bourke the Paper Medicine Man—Crook they called the Gray Fox. It was Bourke who followed Crook in his pursuit of Geronimo and Bourke who wrote a classic account of that memorable chase. The book, *On the Border with Crook,* is fresh and readable today.

John Gregory Bourke went on to pursue his ethnological studies here and there across the West. He produced a study called *Snake Dance of the Moquis of Arizona,* with a fine pictorial cover of the Indians handling snakes. We bid as high as we could afford to go on *Scatological Rites,* but we didn't win.

Marcia and I would have enjoyed spending a week on the third floor of Lowdermilks, just as we would have enjoyed spending more time in the vast fiction room of Acres of Books in Cincinnati, but the time was not to be had.

Getting our purchases out of Lowdermilks was itself a nightmare. There was only one service elevator, and it was always crammed, mostly with government documents bound for the Jenkins Company. I lugged most of our boxes down and stuffed them in my car. I was young then, but even so, the dust nearly got me.

When the Lowdermilks sale ended, Marcia and I were less than a year away from starting our own bookshop.

40

In March of 1971 Booked Up commenced doing business in a tiny shop on Thirty-first Street in Georgetown. We sought, from the first, to be connected in some way with the larger world of book selling, and our first effort in that line was to occasionally indulge ourselves with a trip to New York to attend a fancy auction.

The first such auction we attended was the two-part sale of the collection of William Stockhausen, in 1974. We had been in business more than three years, but took only one bid to that auction. A customer wanted us to secure for him a copy of *Cup of Gold,* John Steinbeck's first book, a biography of the pirate Henry Morgan. We were authorized to go up to $500, and secured the book for $475. We still have the catalogue, annotated by Marcia, but we have long since lost track of our pioneer customer. The money we paid was, at the time, a record price. The book, in fine condition, as ours was, might fetch $40,000 today.

In view of what has come into the auction rooms *since* Stockhausen, his collection seems to have been sort of higgledy-piggledy. Mr. Stockhausen bought whatever caught his eye, which is normal enough. He had some good books, but the collection as a whole lacked snap and the auction itself failed to generate the excitement we had been hoping to feel. Fortunately a chocolate fondue at the Swiss Pavilion restored our spirits.

The Stockhausen sale was followed only three years later (1977) by the three-part sale of the library of Jonathan Goodwin, a Connecticut neighbor of my old teacher Malcolm Cowley, from whose library Jonathan Goodwin coaxed out many treasures, including Faulkner's copy of *The Portable Faulkner,* in which Faulkner had written in mild rebuke that Cowley had deprived him of what he had hoped would be the leisurely occupation of his old age. *The Portable Faulkner* brought $5,000.

The Goodwin sale was a considerably longer affair than the Stockhausen sale had been. The high-end dealer John Fleming immediately bought a book I have regretted not competing for ever since: the dedication copy of Arnold Bennett's *The Old Wives' Tale,* simply inscribed: "From the old man to the old Wife." I like to read Arnold Bennett, Virginia Woolf's strictures notwithstanding, and have acquired—I can't quite say "collected"—some 110 volumes of his work.

Once again Marcia and I journeyed to Park Avenue holding only one commission: from the Houston collector Bing Soph, who lacked, in his excellent E. M. Forster collection, the signed, limited *Passage to India.* We secured it for him for $400—it was the last bid we placed at a major auction until I alone bid futilely at the Peter Hopkirk sale, at Sotheby's London in 1998.

We went to minor auctions on a more or less weekly basis, but— speaking only for myself—I found the major auctions less than compelling. Once you've seen the major players a time or two—John Fleming, Lew David Feldman of the House of El Dieff, Marguerite Cohn from the House of Books Limited, plus someone from Quaritch and maybe someone else from Maggs, or H. P. Kraus or a few others—they cease to be mythic presences and just become businessmen endlessly acquiring books for money, or selling books for money. If we had been rich it might have been fun to play, but we weren't, and it wasn't.

4 I

OUGHT DEALERS TO collect? A good many dealers just don't seem to want to. Lou Weinstein of the Heritage Book Shop (now gone) once showed me his collection of first *American* editions of famous books. My polite view is that Lou Weinstein's heart is not really *in* acquiring books that he can't sell.

The English dealer David Magee, who operated for a long time out of San Francisco, gave it as his opinion that dealers ought to collect *something*, but if possible, something that nobody else really wanted. So he collected Wodehouse, whom nobody wanted then (the seventies) but everyone wants now.

Then there's William Reese, of New Haven, in my opinion the greatest Americanist *ever*, who unabashedly collects American color plate books, many of which are both very pricey and very salable. Bill Reese doesn't care. He got there first and that's that.

At the aforementioned Goodwin sale the collector-dealer Maurice Neville introduced himself to the trade by dominating the first session of the sale, and hanging in there in some force for the two remaining sessions.

In 2004 Maurice Neville toted his treasures back to the salesrooms. Perhaps he had noted the staggering price for modern firsts realized at Robert Rechler's sale the year before. The Goodwin, Rechler, and Neville sales were all, in my opinion, Hemingway-heavy. Must we see, again, the same old Hemingway rarities, inscribed, as it may be, to Sylvia Beach or Don Carlos Guffey (the doctor who delivered Hemingway's sons and who also put these copies in play, to Hemingway's annoyance, in his own sale in 1958)? When will we see these very same copies again, probably in the very same rooms? Those books are now not much more interesting than stock certificates.

To my mind the great sale of 2004 was not the two parts of Maurice Neville's sale but the four parts, sold at Sotheby's London, of the astonishing library of Quentin Keynes. His collection of Richard Burton (the Arabist and traveler) was far more interesting than the same-old-same-old Hemingway, Faulkner, Joyce, and so on.

Quentin Keynes, though, was not interested just in Burton, or Africa: he had amazing Pound, his *second* collection of that worthy, I understand. I read those four catalogues with amazement. Until they came in the mail I had never heard of Quentin Keynes, though I now know that his father was the bibliographer-collector Geoffrey Keynes and his uncle John Maynard Keynes.

42

ONE OF THE intriguing aspects of antiquarian book selling or book collecting is how whole segments of literature—travel books, let's say— suddenly double or triple in value because of one sale. Such a thing occurred in 1998, when the distinguished *Times* of London journalist Peter Hopkirk, who had been everywhere and who had also written seven books about the Great Game—the nineteenth-century rivalry between England and Russia over Central Asia and the route to India—decided, now that the books were written, to sell his travel books at auction.

The best known of his seven books is probably the first one, *Foreign Devils on the Silk Road,* probably because it is about those two famous looters Aurel Stein and Sven Hedin.

Peter Hopkirk was also interested in Dalmatia, the Middle East, and everywhere. He had bought books all over the world and in his introduction to the catalogue, acknowledged the part secondhand book shops had played in his education.

The auction house he chose was Sotheby's. We subscribe to the catalogues of both Sotheby's and Christie's, mainly for their reference value. This time, reading the catalogue and being an admirer of Peter Hopkirk anyway, I decided to make a few bids for a number of travel narratives by women that my own large if disjointed collection of such narratives lacked.

I was fairly flush at the time and I was also convinced that the rarer of the various travel narratives by women might never come my way again, so I shot for the moon. I asked my friend John Saumarez Smith, manager of G. Heywood Hill, the well-known Mayfair bookshop, to go bid for me.

My bids totaled twenty-six thousand pounds, an imprudent amount to cast upon the waters of an auction house.

As it happened, the day of the first session of the Hopkirk sale was one of those days when the world changes. Travel books—for decades if not centuries undervalued—suddenly became very valued. Players with deep pockets showed up, one of them a sheikh who proceeded to sweep the Middle Eastern offerings in toto.

Just as I was beginning to wonder if I had been wise to commit such a vast sum to women runaways (as many women travelers are), the phone rang, and it was John, who informed me that the world had changed and that I had been skunked, shut out, whatever.

The reality proved to be even worse than what John reported: I got one miserable lot by default, and it turned out to be four books by the Gobi-trotting missionaries Mildred Cable and Evangeline and Francesca French. Three of the books I already had. My sole trophy from the brilliant Hopkirk sale was a juvenile called *The Story of Topsy.*

Later I did secure one stray from the Hopkirk collection, a book by the Silk Road explorer Albert von Le Coq, bearing Peter Hopkirk's elegant book label. It came drifting into Archer City from the great firm of Maggs in Berkeley Square.

Peter Hopkirk had wonderful books—they fully merited the prices paid—but I think too that it was lucky for him that the world changed just when it did.

43

THE LEAP FROM scout to dealer is a very significant one. A scout, as the name suggests, is free to roam. Most open-shop dealers continue to roam when they can, but shop pressures usually keep them stationary more than they would like.

Most scouts don't limit themselves to one specialty, since that would severely limit the number of dealers they could sell to. Of course, there are exceptions. The bookseller Brian Kirby, of Glendale, California, scouts mostly movie scripts and movie-related materials. One collector-scout-dealer, Stuart Teitler, indulged his passion for tango while he scoured the earth looking for Utopian and Lost Race fictions. He seemed to manage this balancing act for some decades.

Book scouts remain romantic figures: the very fact that they roam calls up romantic affinities with Kit Carson and Jedediah Smith. None have names that are known to the general public. In his time Ike Brussel was well known to booksellers, but the general public had never heard of him.

In 1952 *The New Yorker* did a piece on the book scout Louis Scher; then, in the seventies, the same magazine did a piece on me. Neither piece made any impression on the populace.

Not too long ago a scout who wishes to be nameless—the preference of most scouts—found, in a shop in Walpole, New Hampshire, a copy of Edgar Allan Poe's *Tamerlane*, a legendary rarity of which, now, twelve copies are known.

Most of us in the rare book business scout when we can.

The scout I know best—he's also the best scout I know—is David Sachs of Oakland, California. Recently we acquired nearly five hundred volumes of Anglo-Indian literature, all scouted up by David, all in fine condition.

David is not unsociable, but mainly, he scouts. By the end of a visit to Booked Up, the seat of David's pants will be unusually dirty, which is because he scoots on his bottom in order to be able to look closely at the lower shelves. Doing the bottom shelves is a discipline few scouts have. David Sachs has it.

Peter Howard of Serendipity Books has often acknowledged David Sachs's help in filling in university want lists of often unprepossessing books.

In a recent visit to Booked Up, David, who has a strong interest in émigré literature, came across a batch of Cuban poetry, some of it by exiles, some of it inscribed. This was David's bread and butter, and he is rarely confounded on his home turf; but he *was* confounded this time by a number of books that had a big fat zero where the price should have been. Why a well-respected dealer, such as the one we got the books from, would price a book zero was beyond David's ken—and come to think of it, beyond mine too. Did it represent the owner's opinion of the poet? Neither of us knew: sometimes booksellers just do odd things.

Scouts are the seed carriers, a vital link to the food chain of book selling. They have the time—as most dealers don't—to inspect junk shops and visit yard sales. At a yard sale in Tucson a complete run of Melville first editions turned up, and it included *The Whale*. They had all been rebound, with the original covers bound in; but even so, they made a book scout's day.

44

LONGTIME BOOKSELLERS RARELY lose their love of scouting: what they lose is the time to scout. Our own store, Booked Up, now contains remnants of the stock of at least twenty-six bookshops. Most of these purchases are sorted, repriced, and put in their proper section, but knowing as we do that some book buyers resent too much organization, we leave a couple of long walls, containing maybe 120,000 books, unsorted, with books that range in price between $10 and $40.

When I am at a loss for what to do next, I find I like to scout my own stock, and I always start with the general shelving.

Recently, in a section of shelves containing mostly books from the stock of the Pennsylvania book dealer Norman Kane, I found, in dust wrapper, a copy of a book never seen by me before. It was called *Mr. Zouch: Superman* and was the ill-titled American edition of Anthony Powell's early novel *From a View to a Death*. It was priced $7.50 and was my all-time best find in our own stock. I repriced it $350 and sold it that afternoon.

In fact we almost never get around to repricing our books—lots of rather desirable ones are still sitting on our shelves, carrying prices that are something like a quarter of a century old. Virtually every catalogue that floats in convinces me that vast areas of our stock are seriously underpriced, and yet it's unlikely that we'll do anything about it. The customers who care to look closely will come away with bargains, and bargains are one of the things that help keep book selling alive.

45

AFTER THE DUST of the Lowdermilks sale settled, Marcia and I began to look for a place to have our bookshop, and we found one on Thirty-first Street in Georgetown. A friend named John Curtis, whom Marcia had worked with in the office of Allard Lowenstein on the Hill, was at loose ends and went in with us for a year, after which he moved to Williamsburg, where, ever since, he has operated an excellent shop called the Bookpress.

We opened with a stock of about a thousand books and perhaps as much as $1,000 in capital. Soon we moved across the street, into less cramped quarters; in time we expanded into a shop that filled nine apartments, on three floors of a building at the corner of Thirty-first and M.

There we stayed, a visible presence in the book world, for thirty-two years.

For the whole term of the business there, Marcia, with her daughter Cecilia, lived about two blocks from the shop.

We were, for some time, an entirely self-capitalized business. From the moment we opened our doors, customers surged in. And eager customers, at that.

James and I were living then in the hamlet of Waterford, about forty miles away but still, in the early seventies, an easy commute: there was only one traffic light between our house and the Key Bridge. Now there are probably thirty, but by the 1980s, James had graduated from prep school (Woodberry Forest) and gone off to make his mark as a singer-songwriter. He will soon be releasing his ninth album, and, it seems to me, his best songs are as good as anyone's best songs. Indeed, I suspect that the mark he has made artistically is more likely to be indelible than the mark I have made. Great songs outlast all but the greatest prose.

With James gone from home it was no longer necessary for me to commute. From 1980 on I lived in a noisy apartment above the shop, and also, unfortunately, above the discos of M Street, which pushed out their rowdy clientele about 2 A.M. I finally got a white noise machine, which, if set on "Waterfall," more or less held its own with the revelers.

46

SUCCESS IN BOOK selling—or anything else—can often be a matter of timing. We opened our shop in a kind of interlude between the dominance of Lowdermilks and the arrival of fresh energies such as the Ahearns (Quill and Brush) and Allan Stypeck (Second Story Books) and a few others, all of them going strong by the mid-seventies.

Though dominant for much of a century, Lowdermilks was never the only bookshop in D.C. Washington was a great world capital, too various to be served by only one bookshop, however great—and for what it's worth, by the time we got to Lowdermilks, it was not great: just large.

One reason I've hung on to book selling is that it's progressive—the opposite of writing, pretty much. Eventually all novelists, if they persist too long, get worse. No reason to name names, since no one is spared. Writing great fiction involves some combination of energy and imagination that cannot be energized or realized forever. Strong talents can simply exhaust their gift, and they do.

Book selling, though, being based on acquired knowledge, *is* progressive. At least, that seems to be the case with the great dealers. The longer they deal and the more they know, the better books they handle.

Not all dealers progress, of course. That dealer in New Hampshire should have known about the *Tamerlane*.

The great dealers—and there will only be a few, in any generation—learn and keep learning.

47

THE FIRST THING Marcia and I did after we opened our shop was to go around and visit the other dealers in town. Nice Mr. Bill King welcomed us to his downtown shop, whose stock was clearly dwindling. Bill King was soon gone.

On Capitol Hill a large, messy bookshop filled with treasures was run by a large, untidy man who slept on a blackened cot between his shelves. Personal comfort meant little to him—the quality of his books meant everything.

In McLean, Virginia, there was a nice retired CIA man whose shop was called the Lost Generation bookshop (there's one with the same name in St. Louis). It was there that I bought the three Eragny Press books inscribed to Franklin Gilliam.

Of course, there were bookshops spread throughout the suburbs, inside and outside the Beltway—we eventually visited all of these, in a kind of hopscotch manner. We were by then assisted in the shop by Mrs. Elizabeth Rice and used her shop days to forage around the area.

The great lady of Washington booksellers then was the formidable Amalya Reifsneider, who ran the Park Bookshop. The shop was born in New York, but ended its days on Nineteenth Street in D.C., next door to the town house of the seer Jean Dixon, who was a good friend of Mrs. Reifsneider, who then numbered among her loyal customers Donald Graham, now CEO of the Washington Post Company. Her stock was particularly rich in historial memoirs—it was largely from the shelves of the Park bookshop that I began to form my collection of memoirs by upper-class ladies, not a few of whom were married to ambassadors and whose books were likely to contain juicy descriptions of long-ago scandals in foreign courts.

48

IN OUR THIRTY-TWO years of street-level book selling in Georgetown we were able to acquire what the not easily pleased New England bookseller Howard Mott called "a beautiful stock, beautifully arranged." In time we bought about 150 personal libraries in D.C., libraries ranging in size from a few hundred books to several thousand. Many of these libraries would have automatically gone to Lowdermilks, had it still been there. But it wasn't.

Weakly capitalized though we were, the word that we paid fair prices for books soon got around. Many of these libraries came from diplomatic families—we enjoyed three years of good buying, with only minimal competition, and much of that came from Howard Wilcox, whose Estate Book Sales was well established. Rumor—or at least gossip—had it that Howard had so many books offered to him that he made a standard offer of four cents a book. If that was refused he went on to his next offering.

I doubt the four-cents-a-book rumor, because, much later, Howard was asked to bid on the excellent library of the lawyer Hugh Cox, which he bought. He told me privately that he would have bid more than $100,000 if that had been necessary.

By this time (the eighties) there were more than forty book dealers in the D.C.–Baltimore area, and sellers could easily pick and choose. Most of them sold to the first dealer who showed up, and often that first dealer was us.

49

IN THE SUMMER of 1971—our first year in business—a great stroke of luck came our way. The family of a deceased collector in College Park, Maryland, called and said they had some books they wanted to sell—and what's more, they were hoping to have them removed immediately.

We later learned that they had first called Capitol Hill Books, but that shop was being moved that day, and one of the movers was our friend John Gach, who later became a dealer himself—nowadays he sells books on psychiatry and psychoanalysis, with a heavy specialty in Freud and Freudiana.

Both my partners were absent that day, so I closed up the shop and left immediately for College Park.

The only reason I even knew where College Park was was that we were fond of scouting a shop called Riverdale Books, which was nearby. Riverdale Books was the East Coast equivalent of that shop in Oakland where all books were a dime. At Riverdale they were likely to climb as high as fifty cents, but most were more like thirty-five cents.

When I found the house in College Park I was at once thrilled with the books that were piled on the floor.

For starters, there were all fifty-two Edgar Rice Burroughs first editions, including a very nice *Tarzan of the Apes*, lacking the now very expensive dust wrapper. A fine *Tarzan of the Apes* in dust wrapper is approaching $100,000 now, though the second book, *The Return of Tarzan*, has a jacket that is far scarcer: it exists in only two copies, last I heard, though that could change.

Besides the Burroughs, there was a good Stephen Crane collection, lacking the rare first book—*Maggie, a Girl of the Streets*—but including several English editions, which we sold at once and have never seen since.

Most surprising of all, though, was a collection of books published by the Chicago firm of Stone and Kimball. There were 396 books published by that firm, a lot more Stone and Kimball than most booksellers will see in a lifetime. The collection was formed by a man named Hartley Sanders; by chance we later owned (and used) his copy of the Stone and Kimball bibliography, which had been done by the Washington, D.C., bookman Sidney Kramer.

Few of the Stone and Kimball books have much to recommend them except their book design, but there are a handful of exceptions, those being Kate Chopin's *The Awakening*, Henry James's *In the Cage*, and Harold Frederic's *The Damnation of Theron Ware*. They also issued a nice set of Poe and one or two Hamlin Garlins that are not bad.

As a capper, once I'd loaded the books, I found not one but two copies of *Weird Tales*, volume I, number 1, a fantasy pulp that was highly sought after at that time. I think Tennessee Williams may have published in it.

50

Buying books in bulk—that is, buying real libraries containing, sometimes, thousands of books—is a special skill, near to alchemy. One looks, one guesses, the point being to make a bid you can live with and that the owner of the books will accept.

Some dealers simply don't like to buy in bulk; some even prefer buying mostly or entirely from the trade. We like buying lots of books, all at once. Just today we bought a thousand, sight unseen, from a dealer we trust.

Not since buying the general stock of the Larry Edmunds bookshop in the sixties had I had to estimate what to pay for a mixed lot of books. (Indeed, I didn't even have to do this with Larry Edmunds because Milt Luboviski told me what he'd take and I accepted his figure immediately.)

Hartley Sanders's books, in College Park, was the first time I had been faced with an enticing jumble for which I needed to come up with an offer. That was not especially hard: we had $1,500 in the bank, and $1,500 was my bid.

To my great relief the offer was immediately accepted. After all, I had shown up. But for luck, Capitol Hill Books would have shown up and probably bid higher, though maybe not.

In fact Hartley Sanders's descendants were tired of having the books on the floor, and probably would have taken less had less been offered.

51

SOMETIMES, FRUSTRATING AS it is for the bookseller, it can be a long while before a collector—or his or her children or grandchildren—decides to let the books go. And whether the offer is $1,000 or $100,000, money is seldom really the decisive factor in a purchase of long-held books. The drama of release belongs to the owner, and it can involve a long overture.

We once bought a fragment of the library of the long-dead theatrical producer Crosby Gaige, most of which had initially been sold to the Scribner's bookshop, when there was one. A young collector, not rich, wandered into Scribner's at this time and was able to buy thirty or forty of Crosby Gaige's best books, including the one-of-one-hundred *Ulysses*, for a rather modest sum. Among them were some excellent Eliot, Frost, and others.

The collector went on to become a schoolteacher in suburban Maryland, where he enjoyed the books for many years.

One day we were invited to come take a look, which we did. Crosby Gaige had morocco slipcovers made for most of his books, varying the color scheme from author to author: brown for Frost, green for Eliot, and so on.

We offered all we had in the bank at the time—and then we waited. For several years we heard nothing.

Then one day the collector called and said, come and get them: he evinced no sadness when we took them away. He had owned those books as long as he wanted to. The release had been a long time coming, but when it came, it was final and it evoked no visible regret. Something was over, and that was that.

52

WE BOUGHT THE College Park books late on a Friday. Somehow book people know when a local dealer makes a big or attractive buy.

General Crook's Crow and Shoshoni scouts are said to have known almost immediately about the disaster at the Little Bighorn in June of 1876—although they were more than one hundred miles to the south.

I unpacked the books at my home, did a hasty sorting, and, the next morning, hauled a hundred volumes or so to the shop, hoping to titillate the Saturday crowd. Though we had been open only a few months, we already had regulars.

I didn't take the Stone and Kimball, nor the Burroughs, but I *did* take the two copies of *Weird Tales,* volume I, number 1.

(Speaking of regulars, there is a nice little memoir of the old Paris *bouquiniste* Gustave David, who moved at some point to Cambridge, England, and established a little stall. As to our shop, regulars promptly came, among them the Keynes brothers, John Maynard and Geoffrey. The latter, though a surgeon by profession, was also an accomplished bibliographer: Blake, Harvey, and others. Gustave David's little stall in Cambridge earned him a modest place in the history of English book selling.)

In our case, we had scarcely got our catch of the day out of my car when a boy who might have been eight walked in, and a stylish lady who might have been forty walked in just behind him. The lady proved to be the boy's aunt, and she very much wanted to buy her visiting nephew a nice present: but what?

Then the boy asked unprompted if we by chance happened to have a copy of *Weird Tales,* volume I, number 1.

Startled, I said that in fact we *did* have a copy of that very issue—in fact we had *two* of them. At the time I had no idea what the magazines were worth, but the aunt said she'd like to buy them both, so I said, how about $600, and she immediately wrote me a check.

The magazines had been in the shop less than ten minutes, and thanks to them, we already had one-third of our money back, which is how antiquarian book selling is supposed to work.

Somewhat shaken by the rapidity of a transaction which had taken me completely by surprise, I was about to price a little book that I had never seen before. It was called *The Fiend's Delight,* by an author called Dod Grile. I had never heard of Dod Grile and was considering a price of $15. Fortunately the very nice and very professional children's book dealer Doris Frohnsdorff happened to be in the shop at the time.

Doris very gently mentioned that Dod Grile was the pseudonym of Ambrose Bierce.

Not every bookseller, with a sleeper about to be ready to hand, would have been that nice.

Sure enough, *The Fiend's Delight* turned out to be the old gringo's first book, and worth a pretty penny.

Our first library was soon paid for, and Booked Up was on its way.

53

THE INSTANT SALE of the two *Weird Tales* was sort of stunning. We had not even had time to look at the table of contents: maybe Lovecraft had contributed, or maybe Robert E. Howard. Still, $600 seemed enough, and still does.

A few days later we sold the Burroughs en bloc for a good price. The Stone and Kimball took longer, but we eventually sold that also, to our impulsive Baltimore neighbor John Gach. Add on the pricey Stephen Crane and we had realized about $10,000 for the Hartley Sanders books, which provided us with a handy bit of capital should opportunity knock again.

Knock it quickly did. A day or two later we were invited to view the books of Dr. Philip Graven, who was one of the first Vienna-trained analysts to practice in Washington, D.C. Dr. Graven had been a Freudian—there was a real analyst couch in his consulting room. Though his books were good, it's the couch that I really wished we had bought; that and the more than fifty pairs of fine handmade gloves that we discovered in a drawer.

Dr. Graven had modestly interesting English books, including a nice *Gatsby*, but the more interesting part of his books—his working library—was in German. Since I had faded out of graduate school before I got to German, I was at sea and so was Marcia, although her father, George McGhee, had once been our ambassador to Bonn.

The German books—possibly packed with Freud first editions—we eventually sold very cheaply to Stan Lewis, a New York dealer with a shop on upper Broadway, which closed after Stan was the victim of a vicious mugging. He continued to deal, but from safer quarters. We sold him Dr. Graven's German books for $600, for the simple reason that that was the most he would give.

In retrospect it seems a little odd that so many psychoanalytical books came our way. A few years later we bought, in installments, the large library of Dr. Rudolph Allers, author of *Successful Error*. He was, I suppose, a Catholic anti-Freudian. The prize of his collection was Hannah Arendt's thesis on St. Augustine—it went quickly to John Gach.

Finally, where psychoanalysis goes, I find it interesting that the last significant library we bought in Washington, D.C., was that of a learned woman, Dr. Winifred Gray Whitman, who was perhaps the first analyst in the capital to specialize in the psychoanalysis of children.

Dr. Whitman had wonderful books, of all sorts. It was in her collection that we acquired the only first edition of *Alcoholics Anonymous* that we have ever owned. It was a beautiful copy and sold for a commensurate price.

54

WORD SOON GOT around that the tiny bookshop on Thirty-first in George-town was a place where one might find interesting books to read, and furthermore, if offered interesting books, Booked Up bought them for good prices.

Customers came, and so did books.

Even Alice Roosevelt Longworth came; she was, of course, the daugh-ter of Theodore Roosevelt and had been something of a social terror in Washington for seven or eight decades.

She wandered in wearing a big floppy hat and bought two mysteries—we were so humble in those days that we kept a whole wall of books priced at $2 each.

Mrs. Longworth was said to be an omnivorous reader, reading far into the night in her big house near Dupont Circle, where she lived with her granddaughter Joanna Sturm.

On two occasions we were invited to buy books from Mrs. Longworth, but neither time did we actually enter her house: the books were brought down and piled in a porte cochere, and Joanna Sturm handled the trans-action. The books were excellent and the arrangement suited us fine.

When Mrs. L. died the remaining books passed into Joanna Sturm's possession—we more or less gave up hope of getting any more, which was wrong. Sooner or later, everything gets sold. The great Chaucer at Chats-worth stayed there for hundreds of years, but finally it got sold, and the same can be said, in spades, for the famous Macclesfield Psalter, which had rested unseen and unsuspected on the very top of a shelf for centuries—until it was found and sold.

Thus it proved to be with Mrs. Longworth's books. One day Joanna Sturm walked into the bookshop and asked if we'd like to buy any more of Granny's books. Of course we would, we said.

It seems—I have no idea whether this is true—that Joanna wanted to buy a BMW motorcycle, cost about $7,500. We happily gave her that amount and I spent a happy day rummaging under stairwells and in closets, until I had a carful more of Mrs. Longworth's books.

One book only I kept. I was reading English political biography, and had become interested in Arthur James Balfour: Lord Salisbury's nephew, darling of the Souls, Conservative prime minister, and spoiler—some say—of Lord Curzon's chance to hold the same job. An enigmatical man, but smart.

Arthur Balfour had come to America during the middle of World War I. There were numerous fancy dinners, at one or more of which Mr. Balfour met Princess Alice, as Mrs. Longworth was then sometimes called. At one such occasion Mr. Balfour gave Princess Alice a copy of some of his speeches, and he inscribed it. The speeches were unreadable: Balfour's eloquence, and he had it, didn't carry into cold print. (Lyndon Johnson had the same problem.)

I have long studied the rivalry between Balfour and Curzon—if I knew enough I'd write a novel about the two rivals.

I *don't*, of course, know enough, and I won't be writing that novel, but I'm very glad to have the little book of speeches that Arthur James Balfour gave to TR's daughter.

55

A FEW YEARS later there was a kind of sequel to our dealings with Alice Roosevelt Longworth. Mrs. Longworth's husband, Nicholas Longworth, once Speaker of the House, had died in 1931, and it turned out that he too had a library—in fact, judging from his books, he was a very well-read man, with lots of books in the areas of literature, history, travel, political biography, and the like.

These books had been in storage in Bethesda, Maryland, for a very long time. On an especially cold day we were called to the warehouse where they were, to buy whatever Joanna Sturm didn't want to keep.

Joanna was assisted in her selection by Selwa ("Lucky") Roosevelt, wife of Archie Roosevelt and, a bit later, head of protocol in the White House of G. H. W. Bush.

Joanna didn't seem to be very interested in Nicholas Longworth's books: perhaps, like ourselves, she was simply frozen. We were rewarded for our endurance by a nice American first of *Moby-Dick*. But otherwise, we mostly took history: Henry Adams, Parkman, Prescott, and the like. I myself was most interested in a two-volume novel called *Merry-Mount*, by John Lothrop Motley, the famous historian of the Dutch Republic.

It seemed to me a keeper and so proved to be. We had it for at least thirty years—in fact, though I haven't seen it lately, I'm not so sure we've sold it yet.

56

ONE OF THE more extraordinary men we've met in our years as booksellers was the polymath Huntington Cairns, who was by turn jurist, philosopher, classicist, editor, anthologist (*The Limits of Art*), and, for many years, secretary to the National Gallery of Art.

One day we got a call from a frequent customer of ours, J. M. ("Mel") Edelstein, who was at that time head librarian of the same great museum.

Mel's call was made on behalf of Huntington Cairns, who had recently had a heart attack. He was old, heavy, and in generally shaky health; he thought he might drop dead any day.

What worried him particularly, with that possibility in mind, was his wife, who was seriously non compos mentis. Somehow she managed to lunch with us at the Cosmos Club, but it was a near thing, and we all knew it.

Huntington Cairns had about sixteen thousand books, spread through many rooms of an old, smoky apartment on California Street. What he hoped was that Marcia and I could appraise the books *that day*: he was giving them to the National Gallery and wanted them moved the next day.

This was a somewhat daunting task. Huntington Cairns had been at the swim of American intellectual life for many years. He had known many writers: Dylan Thomas, Pound, Allen Tate, Alexis Léger (Saint-John Perse), Mencken (whom he edited), and, most closely, Henry Miller, who was constantly sending Huntington books he thought Huntington might like. When, more than a decade later, we had the opportunity to look closely at Huntington's books, we found more than sixty-five books given to Huntington Cairns by Henry Miller—most were inscribed. Some were books Miller had written himself, but many were just books he thought his friend should have.

On the day of our one visit, we didn't know about the inscriptions, and time was short. Mel Edelstein had assured us that we could have the excess, once the National Gallery had sorted out what it wanted to keep. (Twelve years later, as he was departing for Los Angeles to become librarian of the Getty, he made good his promise.)

That promise, of course, was enough to entice us to attempt the appraisal. We launched into a rapid count of the Cairns library. There were 750 books on Plato and Aristotle alone. We eventually got many of these, but the National Gallery did keep Huntington's complete collection of the Loeb Library.

The total we came up with, at the end of a dusty day, was about sixteen thousand books, which we valued at a little over $200,000. It was, of course, a hasty appraisal, complicated by the fact that Huntington had been depreciating his library over the years, but we submitted our appraisal confidently, and the IRS did not dispute it.

The books were indeed removed to the National Gallery the next day. They slumbered for years in a storage facility beneath the new East Building. When the time came to remove them we had to push them in an ant colony of carts all the way to the loading docks beneath the old National Gallery building. (There is a privileged exit from the East Building, I believe, but it is for the likes of the late Princess Diana, or perhaps Queen Noor, but definitely not for book removers.)

Huntington Cairns died at Nags Head, North Carolina, in 1985.

My favorite of all the rarities we got from Huntington Cairns was Henry Miller's own copy of the *I Ching,* twice inscribed by Miller to Huntington Cairns.

Though it seems to me to be the perfect West Coast book, it took nearly a decade to sell.

57

I NOWADAYS HAVE the feeling that not only are most bookmen eccentrics, but even the act they support—reading—is itself an eccentricity now, if a mild one. Interrupted narrative has become a natural thing. One could argue that Dickens and the other popular, serially published nineteenth-century novelists started this, and the television commercial made interruption come to seem normal. But the silicon chip has accelerated the process of interruption beyond all reckoning: iPods, BlackBerrys, laptops all break narrative into shorter and shorter sequences.

Still, it's at least possible that these toys will someday lose their freshness and an old-fashioned thing, the book, will come to hold some interest for the masses again.

Then again, maybe not. Reading itself may have already become a mandarin pursuit—I'm using the term Cyril Connolly adopted years ago in *Enemies of Promise*.

Certainly street-level book selling in a big urban setting will produce many surprises.

One day, idling away the afternoon in our first little cubbyhole bookshop, I was startled to see a bloody foot appear in our doorway. The foot belonged to a homeless girl who had cut herself on a broken wine bottle in the alley beside us. We got her medical attention and she easily survived, after which we learned that she was a descendant of Button Gwinnett, whose signature is the most elusive of all the signers of our Declaration of Independence.

At Booked Up one of our favorite eccentrics was a gentleman we called the "little book" man.

Once or twice a year this customer would show up at the shop with a ruler and work his way around the main room, measuring the books.

He was not cheap in the least, and seemed to have no exact height limit. Every time he showed up he spent $2,000 at least, and often more. He never said much—indeed, I can't recall him saying anything. But he always went away carrying a box of short books.

58

MOST OF THE collectors whose libraries we bought were dead years before the libraries came to us, so the only way we could judge the level of eccentricity in the collectors was the books themselves, or from other evidence. Philip Graven, as I noted earlier, had fifty pairs of fine handmade gloves.

An Orientalist named Paul Linebarger, whose father, we were told, had been Sun Yat-sen's lawyer, had absolutely wonderful books, but he had other things too. He was an early expert at psychological warfare, which I believe he later taught. In one of his closets, for example, we found a huge pile of anticommunist comic books in Mongolian. Paul Linebarger also wrote science fiction, under the name Cordwainer Smith. And he had an interest in ladies' lingerie. One of the more unusual things we bought from his estate was a bra mannequin, complete with bra. Several drawers full of bras we let lie.

Since a high majority of our customers were eccentric to some degree or other, it might be best in this narrative merely to mention a few grand originals who were then still alive.

If that's the plan, who better to start with than Sheri Martinelli, friend and perhaps muse especially of poets: Pound, Cummings, Bukowski. In fact, a selection of her correspondence with Charles Bukowski has been published by Black Sparrow.

We had probably been in the business a little over twenty years when, one day, a nice young woman from West Virginia walked in and came right to the point. Her aunt, Sheri Martinelli, had been a close friend of Ezra Pound and had something like four hundred letters from that difficult master. She was also friends with a number of other writers, among them Cummings and Anaïs Nin. (The niece did not mention Charles Bukowski, who, at the time, was hot as a pistol collecting-wise.)

We were intrigued but hesitant. Of course we would like to buy some of what Sheri Martinelli had for sale, but four hundred Pound letters were way beyond our means; and there was also the likelihood that they would be claimed by Yale, keeper of the Pound estate. (Yale, of course, did know about Sheri and her trove.)

Nonetheless we *were* booksellers and were hopeful of buying something that the young lady's aunt might have for sale.

The niece more than once emphasized her aunt's shyness. Would it be possible for us to meet her some morning before the shop opened?

Of course it was possible, and a date and hour were chosen: a Saturday at 7 A.M.

On the appointed Saturday Marcia and I were in our place.

Sheri Martinelli turned out to be too shy to be prompt, but she *did* come. About eight o'clock the oldest Winnebago I have ever seen came creeping slowly up to the curb. It might have been the first Winnebago to roll off the line. We peered at it and noticed vague movements inside. The better part of an hour passed, and then, to our amazement, Sheri emerged, dressed entirely in black. Her hat was black, as was her heavy veil. Her outfit was very black, and so were her shoes. She looked as if she had stepped out of a Victorian melodrama—or would have except for the exceptional jewelry she wore. Most of it was silver and looked as if it might have come from Zuni, the pueblo most noted for its silver work, a long time ago.

We offered a chair and she took it. Then, in a soft, girlish voice, with no small talk, she began to discuss the Master, whom she had had the temerity to visit not long before. He was writing and was not pleased to see her—I believe he told her to go back where she came from and stay there.

Sheri Martinelli seemed to take this rebuff in stride—after all, she knew the Master's ways. She had been making a special box to house his copy of the *XVI Cantos* and had hoped to show it to him and get his approval, but he was in too sour a mood, so she desisted.

When she left I had the vague sense that I had met her before, possibly in Houston at the home of Del Weniger, who, with his wife, Loujon, had published a little magazine called *The Outsider*, in which her friend Bukowski had appeared. But I'm not sure.

What I am sure of was that Del Weniger was a very nice man, ill cast as a hippie. He was in fact an authority on rattlesnakes, about which he published an impressive study.

In time Sheri Martinelli visited Booked Up once more. On her second visit I was allowed to explore the Winnebago, which smelled of cats and rotting bananas. The Pound letters were stuffed in card boxes.

I left these undisturbed and concentrated on smaller fry: some Cummings letters, the box with the *XVI Cantos* in it—Sheri had by then despaired of getting it into the afterlife—and some odds and ends, including several paperbacks of the works of Anaïs Nin, illustrated ex officio by Sheri. Much of this we were a long time selling, but it was unusual stuff. We were glad to have it.

I was startled when the Black Sparrow edition of Sheri's correspondence with Bukowski appeared. She never mentioned him, nor did anything by him show up in the Winnebago. We have now learned that E. E. Cummings bought her paintings and that Allen Ginsberg was a close friend.

Very likely Sheri had another trove somewhere, but it was Pound who wrote her four hundred letters.

She died in 1996.

59

ONE OF THE best aspects of antiquarian book selling is that it is so educative. You learn about what you've bought after you've bought it, usually, in order to gain some idea of how to price it.

One of the first significant libraries we bought in Washington posed an immediate difficulty. In a cellar up Wisconsin Avenue we were offered a basement full of books on ship design. The books ranged in date from the mid-eighteenth century to the early twentieth; they were about twenty-five hundred in number and we knew absolutely nothing about them, except that we wanted them.

I grew up far inland and the only boat I had ever been on was the Galveston Ferry. I knew nothing at all of the values of nineteenth-century books on ship design—though I knew they were not worthless.

In the world of goods, as I've mentioned earlier, there are often astonishing congruencies. We had had the ship design books only three days when a dealer from Portsmouth, England, walked in and licked his lips with delight. He at once bought about one hundred of the better books, at very helpful prices. The rest of that fine library slowly trickled away.

This brief discussion of some of our earlier purchases is meant to give the reader an idea of how antiquarian book shops get established.

It helps, of course, if the bookshop opens in a city rich in books, as Washington is. Not for nothing is it a great world capital.

It helps, also, if your local competition is not possessed of very deep pockets. Had the same libraries or collections shown up in New York, Chicago, San Francisco, Los Angeles, or a number of other cities, we probably could not have competed successfully for the books.

Although modern American and English literature was what Marcia and I knew best, we never considered being specialists in that or any other field. I think we would soon have been bored selling only one kind of book, even in a category as spacious as modern first editions.

In Tucson, far from our bookshop, I still make a practice of scouting every day, usually at the Bookstop, a shop I have already praised, but cannot praise too much. The last pricey book I bought there was an account in French of a very early trans-Sahara auto rally. It's a wonderful book, but it isn't modern literature.

60

IN MY YEARS as a bookman scores of thousands of attractive books have passed through my hands at Booked Up. And yet, in all that time, we've handled only two indubitably great books: Isaac Newton's *Principia mathematica* and Goya's *Los Desastres de la guerra*.

Warren Howell, the tall, imposing San Francisco book dealer, was in our shop in Georgetown only once, and the only book he pulled off the shelves on his visit was the Newton, a beautiful copy, just arrived; it was the first issue and was bound in vellum: it's probable that the vellum suggests that the copy had been meant for sale on the Continent.

"Is that Jim Newman's copy?" Mr. Howell asked, referring to the well-known mathematical popularizer, editor of a three-volume anthology called *The World of Mathematics*.

It *was* Jim Newman's copy—we had acquired it and a wonderful Strabo from his widow only a few days earlier. We paid $4,000 for the Newton and priced it $10,000, which would have been $8,000 to Warren Howell with his discount. But Warren Howell was in no mood to play; he was fond of taking books on consignment, rather than buying them outright, unless he encountered a great bargain.

Once again our Baltimore colleague John Gach bought the book, and sold it to Quaritch, whence it found its way into the strange collection known as the Garden Ltd., at whose sale it brought $82,250, I believe.

By now it has probably risen even higher. What is interesting, again, is that it went into play, as with the Hopkirk books, just at a moment when the world changed. When we bought the book and put $10,000 on it we thought that we were pricing it very high. It was common enough in the auction rooms and usually brought around $5,000 or $6,000. We doubled our money, which we always like to do, and had no reason to suppose that the book would suddenly shoot up as it did.

A couple of years later we bought a rather tatty and inexpensive bunch of art books, among which were a lot of heavy nineteenth-century albums, some of them almost scrapbooklike. We piled them in a storeroom and did not make haste to get them on the shelf. Most of them were in borderline condition anyway.

Then one day I finally heaved into action and began to price the albums, only, wonder of wonders, to find the Goya nestled in among them. It was a good issue, too; the book is complicated. Our colleague William F. Hale likes complicated books, so we persuaded him to sell it for us, which he did.

61

UNDERLYING ALL THESE adventures was one motive: I never wanted to be without books I wanted to read, and if I could be reading four or five books at the same time, so much the better. With books pouring into the shop almost daily, this was not a hard thing to achieve.

In this period, Archer City was often in my mind. Sooner or later I might end up there: this in fact occurred in 1996. Inevitably we would be driven out of Georgetown by rising rents: why not prepare for this day by creating a book town in Texas?

Our need for enough stock to fill a book town coincided with the beginnings of a downturn in the fortunes of American booksellers generally.

Very soon we began to be offered whole bookshops—or at least substantial portions of large book stocks, as more dealers elected to take their rare, better books home and jettison the general books.

Accordingly, by way of lining my future solitude with books, we bought:

Much of the stock of the Phoenix Book Shop of New York City (acquired at second remove, from Second Story Books)

The stock of the first-editions dealer Paulette Greene, likewise at second remove, from Second Story

Five thousand low-end moderns (low-end being $500 and down) from the Heritage Bookshop, Los Angeles

Three bookshops were from the Phoenix area, to wit:

The Mesa Book Company, Mesa, Arizona, a general stock that filled two semis
The stock of Robert Hecht of Paradise Valley—who had long been a promi-
  nent dealer in natural history—excluding the falconry, which he kept
The stock of Einer Nissula, a dealer from Finland who lives on a bald knob in
  Fountain Valley, probably the most un-Finnish spot on the planet

Finally:

We twice bought the stock of A Book Buyer's Shop in Houston, operated by
  Chester and Christine Dobie
And we bought the stock of Barber's Book Store, in Fort Worth, the very
  shop I had visited on my escape from the track meet

It's worth mentioning that in my young manhood, well before Booked Up, most of the books that came to me were review copies, sent by various book editors for whom I reviewed. My first reviews were written for the *Wichita Falls Times Record News,* whose book page I shared once or twice with the future senator John Tower, who was then teaching at Midwestern University.

By chance the first book I reviewed was *Dr. Zhivago.* I had never heard of Pasternak, but I had, at least, heard of the Russian Revolution. With this shaky background, I did my best.

Once I was back at Rice, the book editor of the *Houston Post,* Diana Hobby, began to send me books. Often she would want omnibus reviews of authors I had never heard of. Thanks to her I came to review—or at least to issue book reports on—a whole generation of rising British writers: P. H. Newby, Alan Sillitoe, Malcolm Bradbury, Iris Murdoch, and others. I was allowed about one hundred words each.

I liked reviewing well enough, but the main attraction, still, was that it brought me free books, at a time when I could not have afforded to buy them.

Later, in Washington, I did weekly reviews, at different times, for both *The Washington Post* and *The Washington Star*.

For the twenty years or so in which I reviewed for newspapers regularly, I mainly reviewed fiction, with now and then a biography or two mixed in. If one adds them up, I suspect I reviewed several hundred novels—or at least I reported on them—and the result was that I burned out as a reader of fiction. The last novel I reviewed was Anne Tyler's *The Accidental Tourist*, which I did for *The New York Times Book Review*.

Later, when I began to write occasionally for *The New York Review of Books*, my editor, Barbara Epstein—how she is missed—used to send me choice bits of fiction—Charles Frazier, Cormac McCarthy—but I knew I couldn't read them, and sent them back.

62

For most of my fifties, what I read for pleasure was travel writing, and the book that introduced me to the pleasures of inspired travel writing was called *Tent Life in Siberia,* by George Kennan—the nineteenth-century George Kennan, a great-uncle, I believe, of the recently deceased George Kennan, the diplomat and historian who bore the same name.

The nineteenth-century George Kennan was a skilled telegrapher. After the initial failure to lay the Atlantic Cable, a number of wealthy men, led, I think, by E. H. Harriman, got up a scheme to put a telegraph line across Arctic Siberia and link us all up.

It didn't work and it didn't need to, because while young George Kennan and his colleagues were wandering around Siberia, the Atlantic Cable *was* laid, and the company Kennan and his friends worked for went out of business.

Kennan's account of his adventures among the wandering nomads of the Siberian Arctic makes very engaging reading; a reprint with an introduction by me was published by Gibbs Smith some years ago.

As it happened, though, Kennan returned to Siberia some years later and made an exhaustive study of the exile system, parent of the gulags. When he set out, accompanied by the artist A. B. Frost, Kennan thought he approved of the exile system, which is why the tsarist authorities let him go when others had been refused.

In fact, though, once he had occasion to see the exile system at close hand, Kennan realized his mistake; when he went home he wrote a two-volume masterpiece called *Siberia and the Exile System,* in my view a great book and certainly one of the most thorough indictments we have of what became the gulags.

Modern reprints of this classic usually confine themselves to the technical stuff: numbers of prisoners, number of miles marched per day, health matters, and so on.

This is important, of course, but it leaves out the many tragic stories the political exiles had to tell; many of their lives and tragedies Kennan profiles in depth. The investigation took years and nearly ruined Kennan's health, but the book is his vindication. Russian suspicion being what it is, it is remarkable that Kennan managed to go where he went and find out what he found out.

He was very impressed by the moral idealism and courage of the political exiles; he was also shocked by the brutishness of the common criminals. Very quickly he came to recognize the dangers of his own position, not to mention that of the exiles who told their stories to him. Many of the women he met had come to Siberia voluntarily, in order to stand by their men.

Kennan, with his freedom of movement, offered the only chance many exiles had to get a word out to their distant loved ones.

For fear that he himself would be searched, he had to deny many requests. Mostly he *was* searched, but even Russians can be inconsistent. Once, fearing search, he threw away a packet of letters he had been entrusted with; but on this occasion he *wasn't* searched, and he felt guilty long afterward.

Siberia and the Exile System is a noble book: noble in the way that few travel books are.

63

ANOTHER TRAVEL NARRATIVE that seems to me to attain a degree of nobility is Wilfred Thesiger's *Arabian Sands*. There is plenty of adventure in *Arabian Sands*, but what Thesiger is really writing about is the tragedy of the passing of the ancient way of life of the desert Bedouin. Very likely Thesiger was in love with his guides, bin Kabina and bin Ghabaisha, but as James Lees-Milne has suggested, the relationships were probably chaste and the book all the more interesting as a result.

Once I began to read travel books for pleasure I learned very early what my limits were. I liked to read about the deserts and the poles; about Central Asia and about the Amazon. With rare exceptions (Custine) I was not much interested in travel books written before 1850.

I should confess, too, that I mostly read English travel books, including all those mentioned in Paul Fussell's *Abroad*. The English have always gone everywhere, and written about it. Many current English travel writers are readable, but in my view the Silver Age began late in the twentieth century. Better Waugh, Robert Byron, Thesiger, Rebecca West, Peter Fleming, Eric Newby, Norman Lewis, and a few others seem better than their current-day descendants: Colin Thubron, Geoffrey Moorhouse, Bruce Chatwin, William Dalrymple, Redmond O'Hanlon, James Fenton, and others. None of them have the force of Thesiger, the malice of Robert Byron, the sweep of Rebecca West, the charm of Newby, or the irony of Waugh.

I admit, though, that I failed badly with three great classics of English travel, these being Doughty's *Travels in Arabia Deserta,* T. E. Lawrence's *Seven Pillars of Wisdom,* and Apsley Cherry-Garrad's *The Worst Journey in the World.* I could not get into, much less through, any of them.

Graham Greene's travel books also leave me cold. So much gloom, so little color or bite.

I find that I prefer Alan Morehead's *The White Nile* and *The Blue Nile* to the extensive narratives of Livingston, Stanley, Burton, Speke, Baker, Mungo Park, and the rest of the Nile explorers.

I cannot read ten lines of any book by Richard Burton, which doesn't prevent my astonishment at the superlative Burton collection formed by the aforementioned Quentin Keynes. Even with every scout in England on the lookout for him, it is still an impressive feat.

64

BRYAN PERKINS, FROM whom we bought Barber's Book Store, in Fort Worth, had, in his last years, an ever-declining neighborhood to cope with—the thought of the crack-crazed killer would not have been hard to conjure up.

As a consequence of this situation, Bryan's attitude toward the casual customer might fairly be described as skeptical. If he should happen to buy a really good book, and he bought many, his response would be to at once put the book in a paper sack, after which he would put the sack under a table, in a dim corner—if the corner wasn't dim enough, Bryan was not above unscrewing the lightbulb.

As a consequence of this practice, in some corners of the shop pitch-blackness prevailed.

I knew Bryan's predilections well. The minute we bought the shop I screwed in many lightbulbs and gathered up and opened all the paper bags I could find. In one of them was a nice copy of Mrs. Calderón de la Barca's *Life in Mexico,* a good book in itself and even better when it was inscribed, as this one happened to be, to General William Tecumseh Sherman.

I mentioned earlier that I have, in my personal library, about two thousand travel narratives by women. Those books represent probably the nearest thing to a "collection," as opposed to merely an accumulation, that I have.

In this regard I should mention that in the two-story book house, to the rear of the main house, are two collections that *are* collections. One is an H. G. Wells collection that numbers slightly more than a thousand volumes. It boasts numerous variants, colonial editions, and the like. The collection was mainly formed by Nina Matheson, of William & Nina Matheson Books, now in Chevy Chase, Maryland. William Matheson, a consummate bookman, is, in the charming Botswana books of Alexander McCall Smith, "late"—meaning not tardy but deceased.

The collection *above* the stairs in the same book house was formed mainly by William Matheson and is a collection of poets' novels: that is, prose writers who also wrote some poetry.

The reason I have these two collections is their detachability. If I were to become "late," as I surely will someday, their sale would not affect the main library much.

The poets' novels number some twenty-six hundred volumes, most of which, I suspect, Bill Matheson scouted up while Nina was attacking the massive Wells project.

My first thought had been to extend the poets' novels back into the nineteenth century. Many nineteenth-century poets wrote novels, including Shelley, though I doubt that his *Zastrossi* is much read today.

Thomas Hardy has readers, though, and he wrote something like seventeen volumes of prose fiction before bitterness over the treatment of *Jude the Obscure* caused him to leave fiction and turn to poetry.

The mere thought of those Hardys was enough to sober me, when it came to the poets' novels. Just getting the Hardy novels would cost a good $150,000—if one could find them.

Though Bill Matheson is "late," Nina Matheson is still at work, selling interesting books in excellent condition.

65

THE CORE COLLECTION of my lady travelers had been formed by a man named Stacey Lloyd, who happened to be Paul Mellon's stepson. It contained most of the desirable eighteenth- and nineteenth-century books, and they were in the right condition.

Later, from the London dealer Bernard Shapero, came the only seventeenth-century book in my collection—two Englishwomen make their way to Malta. (Mr. Shapero, it now seems, whether as shop owner or auctioneer, may end up with the stock of the Heritage Book Shop.)

When I began to read the lady travelers I soon developed favorites: Emily Eden, Amelia Edwards, Ella Maillart, Kate Marsden (*On Sledge and Dogsled to Outcast Siberian Lepers*), Lady Brassey (and her yacht, *Sunbeam*), Mary Kingsley, Susana Moodie, the two Dianas (Agnes Herbert and her cousin Cecily), and more recently, Dervla Murphy, Christina Dodwell, Bettina Selby, and others.

The famous Gertrude Bell usually bores me, and it's only now and then that I can get on with Freya Stark, who, when she was doing radio broadcasts out of Cairo during World War II, was described by someone as having the "voice that breathed over Eden."

Gertrude Bell's rare first book was in the Hopkirk sale: *Shah Na Meh: Persian Pictures*. I bid a lot but didn't come close.

Why, if the author bores me, did I bid a lot? Maybe just because it's a book I've never seen. I bought a copy of her regularly published first book, *The Desert and the Sown*, from Powell's Books in Portland, Oregon, thirty years ago, before I had any notion of collecting lady travelers.

No one claimed book collecting was rational.

66

WITHIN MY LADY travelers collection there are several subcategories that could be carved out.

There could, for example, be a debutante section: *Three Vassar Girls in Europe,* for example, or *Two Dianas in Somaliland.* It's rare that poor women travel in these places. Or there could be a little collection of lady bicyclists: here we put Dervla Murphy, Bettina Selby, and several others.

Taken as a whole, the collection reveals how durable these lady travelers were. Kate Marsden really did dogsled off to visit leper colonies. Susana Moodie *did* rough it in the Canadian bush, and Agnes Martin *did* help run an ostrich farm.

Choice is a mystery.

Despite my respect for Bill Matheson as a bookman and my fondness for at least two poets, I find that I just don't like to read poets' novels, not even the half dozen by poets as able as William Carlos Williams, Philip Larkin, and Sylvia Plath.

Faulkner was right to call himself a failed poet.

Fortunately he was a great novelist. If all we had to consider was his two volumes of verse we wouldn't be talking about William Faulkner today at all.

67

KEEPING ABREAST OF book trade ephemera, in the form of catalogues, book trade magazines, and occasionally a book about the trade, keeps most dealers as occupied as they want to be.

I read a lot of book trade literature in the seventies, as we were getting going. My favorite of these was John Carter's *Taste and Technique in Book-Collecting.* I still like that book, although there have been others more up to date.

Then came a shift. I read a couple of popular books about the Great War—Barbara Tuchman's *The Guns of August* and Robert Massie's *Nicholas and Alexandra,* and I have been reading about the two world wars ever since. The Great War itself was so astonishing, so personality-rich, so ambiguous still, that one could spend a lifetime reading about it and its aftermath.

Once I got sucked in, there has been no stopping. I knew nothing of military history at first, but I've since read Liddell Hart, General Fuller, John Keegan, Niall Ferguson, and various books about Churchill's trouble with his generals in World War II.

Then I worked back from these books to the movers and shakers—English, French, German, Russian—of World War I. There are, of course, multiple biographies of all the major players: Lenin, Stalin, Hitler, Churchill, the Kaiser, and others. Now I'm doing the same for World War II, concentrating at first on Churchill, whose massive history of that war is in six volumes consisting of almost five million words, most of them his. Then there is the new wave of generals: Eisenhower, Montgomery, Rommel, and so on.

Interesting details now and then pop out of the massive narrative. Goering, for example, wore a hairnet while playing tennis.

I will no doubt be occupied with the literature of the two wars for the rest of my life.

The figures who loom largest at this juncture are Churchill and Stalin. In one of Winston Churchill's many quarrels with Stalin, the latter said that history would decide which of us is right. "Yes, and I'll write the history," Churchill replied, which he did. Marshal Stalin was not pleased.

68

WHEN ACCESS TO the Russian archives was finally gained, it resulted in the amplification or alteration of many subjects and many points of view. Many books of a shocking nature began to appear: Robert Conquest's *Harvest of Sorrow,* Anne Applebaum's *Gulag,* and—my favorites—Anthony Beevor's three recent books on great battles of World War II: *Stalingrad, The Fall of Berlin,* and *The Battle for Spain, 1936-1940.* All three are engrossing.

Although I was alive, if young, during World War II, most of my reading is on the first war and not the second. It was not called the Great War for nothing. Perhaps my interest in it is that the figures who held the stage were so oversized: Lloyd George, Asquith, Balfour, Curzon, Kitchener, Wilson and Colonel House, Clemenceau, Lenin, Rasputin, and so on. That two of the English leaders were conducting passionate love affairs while the great guns roared—Asquith with Venetia Stanley and Lloyd George with Frances Stevenson—caught one's attention.

The Great War shattered a high civilization, and perhaps because it was a high civilization, most of the players, cultural or political, could write—among them the diplomats. One of my favorite Great War books is the memoir in three volumes by the French ambassador to Russia M. Paléologue. This experienced diplomat was watching a world collapse, and he knew it.

Another man who knew worlds were collapsing was the British spy-diplomat R. H. Bruce Lockhart, who, in *British Agent,* gives a vivid account of the perils of being in Russia then. Lockhart was consoled, during his most dangerous hours, by Moura Budberg, who, in later and safer life, had a liaison with H. G. Wells.

One reason for keeping the Matheson-formed Wells collection is that Wells had such interesting girlfriends: Rebecca West, Moura Budberg, Dorothy Richardson, Elizabeth von Arnim, and so on.

It's been noted by many that some of the greatest thinkers, artists, writers, and musicians were working at their peak when the Great War came: Freud, Einstein, Russell, Keynes, Wittgenstein, Joyce, Rilke, Virginia Woolf, Matisse, Mahler, Stravinsky, Picasso, Valéry, Yeats, and so on. Hemingway served in it, Faulkner flew. But the war was inexorable: it took the flower of European youth; and took also, in ragged order, the Romanovs, the Hohenzollerns, the Hapsburgs, and eventually, the Ottomans: ancient dynasties gone within a few years.

69

MANY BOOKMEN, AND some of the best among them, rarely, if ever, read. They acquire and they estimate and they sell; they collate, measure, hype. They read catalogues, they look in bibliographies, they submit quotes. But they don't have time to read.

It could be that one of the reasons Marcia and I remained lesser bookmen was that neither of us ever stopped reading. I was, after all, a reader first and a book dealer last. The same is true of Marcia.

New interests suddenly engage one, and can keep one engaged for years. My current interest is in the Rothschilds, about whom there are many books, of which Niall Ferguson's *The House of Rothschild* is so far the most comprehensive.

Perhaps the reason I like those books is that they are so filled with characters: Amschel, the old man of the Frankfort Ghetto; the five sons, the unruly young females, the private courier system, the palaces, the competitors, the eccentric uncles who rode giant tortoises or had their buggies pulled by zebras.

If the financial details become tedious, I skip them, always the reader's privilege. Somerset Maugham abridged ten great novels because, though great, they were, in his view, just too long.

70

I'M PROUD OF my carefully selected twenty-eight-thousand-volume library and am not joking when I say that I regard its formation as one of my most notable achievements.

Yet, when I walk along the rows of bookshelves now, I feel that a distance has opened between me and my books. Some things had happened to diminish the sense of rapport I always had with those books.

This is made all the odder because of my love of rereading. If I once read for adventure, I now read for security. How nice to be able to return to what won't change. *Slowly Down the Ganges,* a wonderful travel book by Eric Newby, I've now read many times. I also like his funniest book, *A Short Walk in the Hindu Kush,* a book Evelyn Waugh admired very much—and justly.

I think sometimes that I'm angry with my library because I know that I can't reread it all. I would like to, but the time is not there. It is this, I think, that produces the slight sense of alienation that I feel when I'm together with my books now. They need to find other readers soon— ideally they will be my son and grandson, but if not them, other book lovers.

Walking past my long shelves of English literature now, I feel rather like I felt while walking on the Rice campus. A young woman I had long ago dated briefly but intensely came walking up to me with a baby in her arms. She stopped, we chatted pleasantly; then we both walked on, having enjoyed our light encounter.

That's the way I feel now, when among my books. I might pull down a volume of Stevie Smith, read a poem or two, then put the book back and move on. Once I was passionate about Stevie Smith—but when I look into her now, it's a light encounter. And so life moves along.

71

IN MY BIG prairie-style mansion in Archer City I have all manner of *objets* acquired while buying libraries or otherwise book hunting.

One thing I don't have is a narwhal tusk, though we once bought an estate in which one could be found. This tusk was even inscribed to Admiral Peary. On its way to auction the tusk got broken, which is a shame. I mourn its loss just as I regret my inability to acquire a marvelous fly-catching machine made in central Texas, a machine which is described fully in *Cadillac Jack,* my novel about scouting.

What I attempted to do in *Cadillac Jack* was to give some legitimacy to the relationships people have with their objects. Now the Metropolitan Museum, in New York, has recently opened its new classical galleries, to great acclaim. The busts, statues, and sculptures found in those splendid galleries are objects too—many of them just happen to be great objects.

My own objects—I don't consider books to be objects—were picked up willy-nilly in our search for books. Marcia bought a great Buffalo Bill poster, and some Apache basketry that is very valuable now. I have a Sumatran village drum, an Ethiopian triptych, and a great Maori war club, not to mention half of the last buffalo killed in Arizona Territory.

Many oddities come the way of those who live in the world of traders. I secured a fine skull collection from a dealer in Philadelphia, who had acquired the skulls when the anatomy lab closed at Penn.

Mostly I get my odd objects at small auctions in the Washington-Baltimore area. In our early days Marcia and I journeyed regularly to the Harris auction galleries in Baltimore—this was well before the glamorous Inner Harbor went some way toward making Baltimore less slumlike, if not less gang ridden.

The Harris auctions were held in a grimy building on Howard Street. Not far down the street was a book dealer who believed in making all book repairs with duct tape. We didn't buy very much from him.

We almost always came away with something from the Harris auctions, but if pickings were slim, we could always console ourselves with a few first-rate crab cakes from one or another of the area's many restaurants.

I remember particularly one night in Baltimore when Peter Howard and I did some whirlwind book business on the sidewalk outside the restaurant. It was late at night—Norman and Michal Kane, book dealers from Pennsylvania, happened to be there. Why we were doing business on a chancy street in Baltimore at midnight I don't remember. I do remember pricing a lot of poetry books quickly and adding them up in my head until the figure of $4,000 was reached. Peter handed me a check and drove off. The Kanes seemed to find this way of doing business a little irregular, but the deal went down and nobody got mugged.

Another auction house that we visited almost weekly was Weschler's, in downtown D.C., across the street from the hideous new FBI building. The Weschlers cleared estates; they were there to dispose of whatever there was to dispose of, from lawn mowers to French furniture, though if the French furniture was really good it would be saved for one of the firm's intermittent catalogue auctions.

In the weekly auctions of mostly low-end merchandise one could sometimes bingo. Our young colleague Bill Hale happened to snag at a hodge-podge auction sale a truly rare inscribed copy of *The Celebrated Jumping Frog of Calaveras County*, Mark Twain's first book.

The copy went on to become one of the adornments of Maurice Neville's sale in 2004.

I've gone on about auctions to the extent that I have because they work, and the reason they work is human competitiveness. People buy books and many other things at auctions for prices that far exceed what comparable copies would cost from a professional bookman.

I think this because I myself can get irrationally competitive at auctions. Besides the stirring up of one's innate competitiveness, there is also the thrill of immediacy, and the thrill of immediacy is no small thrill. There the book is, or the vase, or whatever. You can buy it, stuff it in the car, and take it home, or to the shop, or to Texas or anywhere.

Often it's a possibility that is hard to resist.

72

As I MENTIONED earlier, in the sixties I became interested in the writer Gershon Legman, author of the brilliant polemic *Love and Death.* The Legman family then lived in an old Knights Templar monastery, La Clé des Champs, in Valbonne, Alpes-Maritimes, France. Valbonne is about twenty minutes uphill from Nice.

As the reader may remember, I had ventured to write Legman about my unusual hardbound copy of *Love and Death.*

In my initial letter I happened to mention that I was a novelist—I even, foolishly, sent Legman a copy of my second novel, *Leaving Cheyenne,* and I inscribed it. Legman immediately fired back a letter informing me that fiction was shit, after which our correspondence lapsed for about ten years. (That copy of *Leaving Cheyenne,* by the way, has been on sale on the West Coast for several years. Legman didn't want it and neither does anyone else.)

G. Legman, bibliographer, folklorist, historian (of the Knights Templar), and wide-ranging student of erotic literature, remained intellectually on the move. Just yesterday I had occasion to recommend *The Horn Book,* his book of studies of folklore and erotic bibliography—a very entertaining and informative book.

Legman has had many arguments, about many theories, with many scholars or would-be scholars—what no one can ever plausibly say is that he was a dull writer or a dull man. On a brief teaching gig in San Diego he became probably the only bookseller-professor to issue a catalogue of erotic materials on the letterhead of an American English department. (I have never seen this list, though I have seen a list of desiderata that he issued from his home in France.)

After our bad start, Legman and I got on friendly terms as the result of an auction. It was a frustrating auction, from the point of view of a bookseller, and it was held in Vienna, Virginia. The firm that auctioned the books normally auctioned furniture, and they showed little interest in the amenities of book selling. Sets were split willy-nilly among various lots.

What this particular collector had, mostly, was erotica and occulta. There we got a nice set of Aleister Crowley's *Equinox,* as well as a good many books on the Great Pyramid and other psychically powerful sites.

Mainly, though, from this auction, we got dirty books, most of them published in America during the Depression. The man whose estate was being auctioned had in fact been a publisher of American erotica, and a significant one: Legman knew all about him. Indeed, Legman seemed to know everything there was to know about American erotica of the Depression era.

I knew that Legman collected erotic doggerel, and I wormed my way into his good graces by sending him several handwritten volumes of homemade sexy verse.

As I was trying to pack my car that sleety day in Vienna, the lawyer for the estate drove up in a car full of what in my high school days were called fuck books. These little booklets were sold in filling stations for a quarter and worked by the flip-the-page method also used in Big Little Books. By flipping the pages the reader-spectator was rewarded with a crude sense of movement.

The lawyer asked if I was interested in the fuck books, and I said I was but could not buy them then and there because—as was obvious—my car was full. We agreed to meet the next day, but he never showed up. He no doubt sold the fuck books immediately to someone with more trunk space.

When Legman got wind of this he beseeched me to track down the lawyer at all cost, and I tried, to no avail.

Some years later we purchased the very fine high-end collection of erotica formed by a gentleman named Benny R. Jones, who had been "late," in the Botswanian sense, for about forty years. This collection, too, contained another batch of erotic doggerel, probably the least expensive items in the Benny R. Jones collection.

These, of course, I sent to Legman, after which our correspondence flowered. He was then at work on his erotic autobiography, called *Peregrine Penis,* in which he becomes his own Casanova. The book was to be very long and very thorough. I got to read only six hundred pages of it, but I can attest to the fact that it was thorough.

I agreed to be a patron of *Peregrine Penis* and sent Legman a little start-up money: we are in the eighties now. At some point he mentioned that he might have to sell his library. He and Judith Legman, his second wife (they have two sons), were land rich but, due to various French restrictions, cash poor.

That was certainly not exceptional: many book people, whatever their status, are apt to find themselves cash poor.

I think I realized, even from across the Atlantic, that G. Legman was not really likely to sell me his famous library, but once invited to Valbonne, I went, mainly just to meet the man.

Judith Legman had once been Judith Davis, daughter of Henry Davis, a San Francisco bookman whose Porpoise Bookshop I had often visited.

I made my way across the sea to Paris, and then down to Nice. After resting for a night at the Hotel du Cap, one of the most beautifully situated hotels in the world, I drove the next morning up to Valbonne.

Once we introduced ourselves, Gershon and I left almost at once for Cannes, which was nearby. On the way we passed one of Picasso's homes—or perhaps it was one of Charlie Chaplin's.

The point of going to Cannes was the need for a Xerox facility, there being none in Valbonne. Gershon and I moped around this famous movie-festival town while the copying machine slowly ground out the six hundred pages so far written of *Peregrine Penis.*

Back in Valbonne, with our immense pile of pages, Judith cooked us a wonderful meal, after which I was installed in a comfortable guest house and left with *Peregrine Penis.* I got through perhaps one hundred pages before nodding off. The next morning I woke up early and read on. Gershon's plan was to publish a mere ten copies of his book: one for him, one for me, and the other eight for selected copyright libraries around the world. In discussing the book I was as complimentary as I could be, but I don't think my praise convinced Legman. After all, he should realize as well as anybody that reading about "the old in-and-out," as Anthony Burgess called it, does have a tedious side.

I made up for any lack of fire by offering to buy the Legmans lunch, wondering, meanwhile, if I was even going to see the books.

Gershon finally led me, rather grimly, down to the house where the books were kept. Body language says a lot—so much indeed that I knew long before we got to the library that Legman didn't really want me handling his books, much less did he want to sell them. Once in the room I noticed that blankets had been draped over shelves, furniture put in front of the shelves; in cases holding the smaller books the volumes were double- or triple-shelved. I did just manage to note that Legman had a world-class collection of jest books. Then, dipping into the files of his vast correspondence, he showed me a photograph of two smirking Dallas policemen holding up the scope-sighted rifle that had allegedly been used to kill John F. Kennedy.

This awkward visit to the book room over, the Legmans and I enjoyed an excellent lunch. I agreed to keep subsidizing *Peregrine Penis,* after which one of the Legmans' nice sons drove me back to Nice, where I stayed in the not-particularly-comfortable hotel where Chekhov wrote *The Three Sisters.*

The Legman library is, as far as I know, still in Valbonne. Judith Legman was cataloguing it, last I heard. Gershon did a brilliant introduction to Patrick Kearney's catalogue of the Private Case (meaning the erotica) in the British Library. In the introduction G. Legman pursued various arguments and theories that he had long pursued.

The last time I heard from him he was quite excited: a near miracle had occurred. The absolute touchstone of European erotica was Pietro Aretino's *Sonetti lussuriosi*, published in Venice in 1527, with sixteen woodcuts by Giulio Romano. The woodcuts, of course, illustrated various sexual positions.

The woodcuts and the sonnets had been known from later editions, but no copy of the original edition had ever come to light. Then the near miracle occurred: a copy of the book was found in Milan, with fourteen of the sixteen woodcuts intact. (I still don't know the details of this discovery.)

Gershon, assuming from my modest patronage that I had a lot of money, wanted me to buy the Aretino, whereupon we would reprint it, with an introduction by himself.

This happy event did not come to pass. The Aretino, once discovered, kept on the move. Quaritch had it for a time; then, I believe, it went into the collection of Walter Toscanini.

Legman had a stroke. I found myself back in Nice and might have visited but was told by Judith that Gershon no longer wanted to be seen by those who had known him in his healthier days.

Gershon Legman was an exceptional writer. I hope there will be a biography, and a good one. Few can have known as much as he did about erotic literature, on both a local and a world scale. He worked with Dr. Kinsey but, as far as I know, left no serious account of his dealings with the man.

He seems, at one point, to have been a kind of agent, helping Henry Miller and Anaïs Nin sell hot-off-the-typewriter erotica in weekly installments to the strange millionaire in Ardmore, Oklahoma, who left these writings in a filing cabinet in his oil company office. The millionaire died and somebody got the contents of that filing cabinet—Legman would probably have known who.

An aspect of G. Legman's work that has gone almost unnoticed is his editorial labors. He edited, for one thing, an excellent collection called *The Limerick.* He had long concerned himself with the various editions of Robert Burns's *The Merry Muses of Caledonia.* He introduced and helped get back in print the Hungarian folklore journal *Kryptadia.* And I believe he helped Jack Brussel (brother of Ike Brussel, the book scout) reprint the three volumes of Pisanus Fraxi's description of his own collection of Victorian erotica. The reprint is squat and unappealing, whereas the three original volumes are very handsome books. All three were in the Benny R. Jones collection, and I kept them.

G. Legman died in 1999. Of *Peregrine Penis* I have heard no more.

73

THE ANTIQUARIAN BOOK trade is healthily cannibalistic. Dealers constantly munch on one another's stocks. In some years more than half our gross sales come from dealers. Many of them are English dealers.

Washington, D.C., is an Anglophilic city—lots and lots of British dealers come through, or used to. Most of them were in Washington to sell books to one or another of the several important libraries in town: the Library of Congress, the Folger, the National Gallery, the Freer, and so forth.

Once we moved into larger and more handsome quarters across Thirty-first Street, the dealers began to pour in. Our shop looked the way many English bookshops used to look, and our books were the sort of books once commonly available in English shops: literature, history, art, sport (in the English sense, which means field sports), horses, gardens, color plate books, cookery, travel, and the like.

Also, our prices were low. In times when the dollar weakened against the pound, as it often did, the English dealers hardly bothered to look at the prices in our books: they just piled up what they wanted. We didn't mind. We were even flattered that these gents would take an interest in our stock.

The first time I noticed the importance of exchange rates involved our friend John Saumarez Smith, managing director of G. Heywood Hill, a shop in Mayfair which sells both new and old books.

John, on what soon became annual visits, stayed just up the road with David and Evangeline Bruce—in fact it was John who informed Ambassador Bruce that there was a shop a few blocks from his house that he might want to check out.

David Bruce did come to our store twice, but he bought no books. In fact it was the other way around, because, over time, we bought more than one thousand books that had once been his.

Our slow accumulation of Bruce books will require a chapter. What I'm concerned with now is the effect of exchange rates.

At the time of John Saumarez Smith's first visit we had just bought an excellent library from a somewhat crusty retired diplomat with a younger and very beautiful wife. In a room on a lower floor there was at least a million dollars' worth of bird books, but these belonged to the diplomat's former wife. We were not allowed to touch them. Still, we bought a carful of very nice books—though I remember with longing the nice book we didn't get: a beautiful copy of T. E. Lawrence's *Seven Pillars of Wisdom*, a fifty-thousand-dollar book these days.

In the books we did get was an expensive fine-press book illustrated by Rex Whistler. It may be that it was *Gulliver's Travels*, but I recall that we put a stiff price on it: $2,000 or maybe more.

John pulled the book down and looked at it two or three times, but he seemed a little doubtful about the price and reluctantly put it back.

On his next visit, a year later, the exchange rates had shifted into his favor and he bought the Whistler book without a moment's hesitation.

74

EMBOLDENED BY OUR first year and a half in the book trade, Marcia and I decided to reward ourselves with a buying trip to England. Marcia, from an ambassadorial family, had been abroad often, but except for a brief trip to Mexico City, I had never been out of the country.

I was about to publish my fifth novel, *All My Friends Are Going to Be Strangers.* My editor, then and now, Michael Korda, had talked to me about his famous uncle Alexander Korda, who had once lived on the whole top floor of Claridge's Hotel.

Marcia and I didn't need a whole floor, but we did stay at Claridge's, where I have mostly stayed ever since.

We were awhile learning the ways of English bookmen—or at least London bookmen. Full understanding didn't come on this first trip. We had heard of a booksellers' street called Cecil Court, where such dealers as Harold Mortlake and William Fletcher had their shops. So they did, but what was in their shops seemed to be mostly junk. We made a few modest purchases and paid for them, a practice we repeated several times through the years. Then one day, at Mortlake's, someone muttered that they did have a few books downstairs. So, into the basement we went, only to be staggered at the sight of thousands of good books that, by our patience, we had earned the right to see.

In the country this trial period was not required—the country dealers didn't want to miss a sale.

Nor was the let's-see-if-they're-patient method universally practiced in London. When we visited the great firm of Maggs we were taken right to the books, and the same was true at Francis Edwards, then occupying, I believe, the only building in England that had been built to contain a bookshop. And a fine one it was.

We didn't know of Heywood Hill at this time, nor did we know John Saumarez Smith, but a few years later I began ordering all my new books from John, mainly because I like English bookmaking better than I like American bookmaking.

Our intent was to go west into Somerset and then detrain to Scotland from Bristol. Our first stop in Somerset was at Michael Lewis's, whose modest but appealing catalogues had been tempting me for years. It was from him that I got my copy of *Garbo and the Night Watchman,* a really hot book in Hollywood at the time, I don't know why, since it's only a fairly pedestrian collection of movie articles, edited by Alistair Cooke.

In fact, on our ambitious tour, fear of the highway brought on by having to drive on what felt like the wrong side of the road kept me from even thinking much about books.

Left-side traffic was not a problem just for me. The experienced Londoner Marguerite Cohn, of the House of Books, Ltd, looked the wrong way in London and was killed by a taxi. Another victim was J. Carter Brown, longtime director of our National Gallery of Art. He too had lots of experience driving in England, but nonetheless drifted onto the wrong side of the road and was in a bad smashup.

Besides London, we bought books in Portsmouth, Salisbury, Bristol, Oxford, Cheltenham, and Edinburgh. Anthony Newnham told us to be sure to visit Alan Hancock, in Cheltenham, which we did, acquiring some forty-five books by Leslie Stephens, father of Virginia Woolf. The forty-five volumes snoozed on our shelves in Georgetown for more than a decade, after which I took them home and read most of them. He was not the genius his daughter was, but his *Hours in a Library* still reads well today.

75

WORSE EVEN THAN the roundabouts, on that first trip through England, was fear of not getting where we were going in time to eat. The rigidity with which the English, in those long-ago days, observed the eating hours was a shock to postcolonials such as ourselves.

Marcia was then a believer in good food guides, one of which was seldom far from her hand. In Italy or France these might have served her well, but in England the guides failed us time after time. Once we missed lunch by ten minutes in a highly rated restaurant near the small town of Priddy. As a result of our laggardliness I have to this day never eaten a priddy oogie, which is evidently some kind of meat pie cooked in a heavy crust that miners could stuff in their pockets and lunch on far below.

In the main we were travelers in an antique land and we didn't know the rules. We arrived late in Bath and were forced to make do with Indian takeout, and even that was obtained only after a long trot down the road.

Once we got to Edinburgh it was evident that we had entered a somber culture. Once I ate alone at a little pub near McNaughton's Bookshop. It was a sit-where-you-can place, and a young couple soon sat themselves at my table. I can't say they made themselves comfortable.

I myself was eating modestly enough: a hamburger steak. The young couple merely ordered rolls. It seems they had walked in from the country to see the military tattoo being held that day at the castle.

Their all but silent debate was whether they could afford to have butter with their rolls.

The young woman was hopeful, but the young man adamant. They had their rolls without butter.

I could not then really enjoy my hamburger steak, but I ate every bite.

76

ONE OF THE skills an urban bookseller—or any antiquarian book seller—needs to cultivate is how to deal with rich people, and here I think some distinction needs to be made between the rich—even the absurdly rich, who abound today—and the monied. It was some years after I moved to the East Coast before I understood the difference between being rich and being monied: old money as opposed to new money is what I am talking about.

In Texas, where I grew up, there were many rich but few monied. When I was at Rice there was a fenced-in neighborhood across the street called Shadyside. A good part of old-money Houston lived in Shadyside: this included Oveta Culp Hobby and the family of James Baker III. River Oaks was flashier and better known, but old money doesn't need—or want—to be better known. Eventually the Memorial district became flashier still, but never as monied.

In Georgetown, merely by keeping my eyes open, I began to see the monied at their sports. Every afternoon, at a certain time, I could walk up one block to N Street and see Pamela Digby Churchill Hayward Harriman accompanying old Governor Averell Harriman on his constitutional. The Harrimans then owned two houses side by side on N Street—a house for the art and a house for themselves.

Pamela Harriman, of course, had many rich and famous lovers—one of them, Baron Guy de Rothschild, just died.

Averell Harriman, by virtue of being E. H. Harriman's son, lived among the monied and the powerful all his life. He traveled with Churchill and Roosevelt, jousted with Stalin, and also with the journalist Sally Quinn, who, when a guest at dinner at his home, refused to excuse herself and retire with the other ladies when the sexes traditionally split after dinner.

Harriman unfortunately had no books to sell, but we acquired a few of his mother's books from a local charity sale.

The most extreme example in our book-selling career of how tricky it can be to buy from the monied involved Janet Auchincloss, Jacqueline Kennedy Onassis's mother, who lived during the latter part of her marriage to Hugh Dudley (always shortened to Hughdie) Auchincloss in a house just two blocks from our bookshop and less than a block from where Marcia lived.

We were invited to come take a look at what remained of Hughdie Auchincloss's library, Yale having been granted first pick. That university, of course, had treasures in such plenty that they didn't lighten the shelves very much. Many of the books Yale didn't want seemed like prime treasures to us.

The ever-practical Janet Auchincloss had already equipped herself with a new beau—I believe she was working down from a fairly long list. Old boyfriends who had known her as a deb might, if still alive and kicking, have their hour.

This particular suitor, who was perfectly nice, was also, like Janet (we thought), of a practical bent. He had a legal pad and a pen and looked as if he were not only willing but eager to entertain offers.

For our part, we were just as eager to make offers and would have; but to our dismay, a complex social mechanism brought matters to a halt. Mrs A. said several times that she just didn't know what to do with Hughdie's books—after we piped up and said as emphatically as we could that we'd be more than happy to take them off her hands. Our shop, after all, was only two blocks away.

It was understood by Janet Auchincloss that *I* must be what for long was called "in trade." The problem was Marcia.

Neither Marcia nor her mother, Ceil McGhee, were really friends with Janet Auchincloss, but socially Washington is a fairly small town, so that, naturally, the three would sometimes end up at the same charity functions, charitable, diplomatic, whatever. Marcia was, in a small way, a person Mrs. A. knew socially, and Mrs. A. could simply not accept that a person she knew socially was "in trade." This was the 1980s, but Janet Auchincloss, for one, was simply not going to acknowledge that the rules had changed.

And that seemed to be that.

We were stumped, sort of, and so was the new beau, who was purely flabbergasted by this turn of events. He had his pad, he had his pen, he wanted to write down offers. *He* knew perfectly well that the rules had changed—the only point of our being there at all was to conduct "trade."

Was his fiancée mad? he must briefly have allowed himself to think. Our car was parked at the curb with its trunk open. There were excellent books there that we were eager to pay for and haul off. What was Janet's hangup?

Well, that was plain, though not simple: Janet Auchincloss did not associate socially with tradespeople. Possibly the butler or the farm manager could do that, but not the lady of the house.

Fortunately for us the new beau was not easily discouraged. The next day we were invited back. Janet Auchincloss was nowhere to be seen. Fearing that she might suddenly pop in we made many offers, filled the car with books, wrote the check, and beat it out of there.

It had been a near thing, though. Had the suitor been less aggressive the books would probably have been given to a charity sale. It would have cost Janet Auchincloss money but at least the rules that governed "society" would not have been traduced.

77

IN 1972, THANKS to the success of the movie version of my novel *The Last Picture Show*, I became, briefly, a hot item on the Georgetown dinner party circuit. After all, Jack Kroll, then the influential film critic for *Newsweek* magazine, suggested that *The Last Picture Show* might be the best American movie since *Citizen Kane*. The best American movie since *Citizen Kane*? Wow! And there I was, helping to run a small bookshop on Thirty-first Street. People of status began to ask me to dinner parties, usually mentioning that the dinner was very informal—I should just wear my Levi's.

Just wear my Levi's? No thanks. I attended maybe five dinner parties, always wearing a suit, which is what the other male guests were wearing.

In three months my fame ended, as the movie was crowded out by other movies. Throughout the next twenty years my social viability rose and fell according to the success, not of my books, but of my movies. When *Terms of Endearment* won Best Picture in the Oscarcade of 1983, I once again soared briefly; the same thing happened when *Lonesome Dove*, the miniseries made from the book of the same name, reaped big ratings for CBS in 1989.

Long before this I had seen through the Georgetown setup, such as it was. Washington is a civil service town in which the stars are not the politicians or the bureaucrats: the stars in D.C. are the journalists. In my time the major players were Joe Kraft, Joe Alsop, Ben Bradlee, Katharine

Graham, Bob Woodward and Carl Bernstein, I. F. Stone, David Halberstam, Neil Sheehan, my Texas friend Larry L. King, Barbara Howar, Henry Fairlie, Willie Morris (occasionally), Evans and Novak, and others.

A world in which journalists are stars is not my world. What depressed me most in D.C. was that the various great houses I was invited to contained so few books. (Joe Alsop was the exception—he had a three-story house filled with books, and he had read them.)

In our thirty-two years in Georgetown we sold only one real book to a member of Congress. Senator Charles Mathias of Maryland bought a very fine Gibbon from us, and he read it. Otherwise the only sale we made to a member of Congress was a four-dollar book on cartooning which we sold to the late-arriving Texas congressman Bob Eckhardt, who aspired to be a cartoonist.

Gary Hart, pre- and post-Donna Rice, often browsed, but I don't recall that he bought. And John Brademas, the liberal congressman from Indiana who was swept away by the Reagan Revolution, brooded over a volume of Lorca once or twice, but I don't recall that he bought it.

78

IF THERE WAS a true reader in Washington, after Joe Alsop and myself, it was probably the distinguished diplomat David K. E. Bruce, who scattered thousands of books among at least three residences, one of them only a few blocks from our shop.

Ambassador Bruce made the news one time—he may then have been our envoy to Beijing—because he arrived at National (now Reagan) Airport and attempted to rent a car, only to be refused because, though he had plenty of cash, he had no credit card. While Ambassador Bruce had been away serving his country, all the car rental companies had gone plastic.

Many people who recognized him were horrified and tried to intercede on his behalf, how successfully I'm not sure.

Looking back on the incident I'm surprised that he even carried cash. American aristocrats, such few as there were, rarely carried money.

Our own good customer Gilbert Harrison, once editor-owner of *The New Republic*, didn't often carry cash. Gilbert would visit our shop every Saturday morning, select a few books, and then go on his rounds, next stop being the produce market on Wisconsin Avenue.

Soon enough his man, black in this case, came along and paid for whatever Gilbert Harrison had selected. I was once in the Harrison home, a few blocks up the street, and noticed a shelf that contained about twenty copies of *The Great Gatsby*.

"It's the book I like to give away," Gilbert said. Then he showed me a copy inscribed to Fitzgerald's mother. "That one I don't give away," Gilbert added. (I think that copy made it into the auction rooms, although it may be that Fitzgerald inscribed more than one copy to his mother.)

Once, years later, Marcia and I attended a farewell dinner for Nancy Harrison, Gilbert's wife. The dinner was held at the surburban home of Michael and Nina Straight: except for Nina Straight, we seemed to be the only people there who had not been in the OSS. The reason it was a farewell dinner was that Nancy Harrison was dying. Among the old OSS hands was the great classicist Bernard Knox and his wife, the novelist Bianca Van Orden.

We ourselves, having no idea why we had been invited, were bewildered and contributed nothing to the conversation, as was likely to be the case the few times I saw the Straights socially.

On one occasion I was invited to their house on N Street, opposite the Harrimans, to meet the new literary editor of *The New Republic,* Roger Rosenblatt. The Straights had moved out of their mansion by then—the introduction was made in a vast room, empty except for a card table, four chairs, and a champagne bucket with a bottle in it. And four glasses, of course, which were not wasted.

The rich are different from you and me, and it's not merely, Mr. Hemingway, that they have more money. It's that they live by a different code, particularly if they're monied and not merely rich.

79

DAVID K. E. Bruce was, I suppose, about as well born as it's possible for an American to be. His wife, Evangeline (called Vangy by her intimates, of which I was not one), had by far the most celebrated salon in Washington during my years there. I was invited a couple of times and went, recognizing that salons organized by great society ladies (remember Proust?), gatherings at which important people from the government, business, or the arts mingled and exchanged pleasantries, would very soon be a thing of the past. I would have been a fool to decline Evangeline's invitations, and I didn't.

At her brunches she liked to serve quails' eggs (good) and honey-soaked bacon (bad).

The one time I went to dinner at Evangeline's house (David Bruce was "late" by then), the guests of honor, more or less, were Roy Jenkins, a jovial enough English pol, and Conrad Black, the tycoon recently convicted of fraud at a trial in Chicago. Lord Black is now, I believe, in jail, but, hey! what's a salon without a rogue or two?

Unfortunately my visits to Evangeline's salons told me nothing about the Bruce books, which were upstairs. I knew, however, that David Bruce read a lot of history, because I often picked up books with his neat signature in them at various local charity sales.

My appetite was whetted by John Saumarez Smith's frequent visits. He stayed with the Bruces and would occasionally avail himself of packing privileges at Booked Up. John got many fine books from the Bruces, but once international postal rates began their ominous rise, a lot of the books the Bruces owned did not justify the cost of getting them home to Mayfair. Many of these books eventually came to us, but the story of how we got them is a long and torturous one.

One night Marcia and I dined with Stephen Massey, then with the book department of Christie's auction house. With us that evening also was Willis Van Devanter, a ubiquitous bookman who had been, for a time, private librarian to Paul Mellon. Private librarians are an elite and very small class. At no time in my career have there been as many as ten operating in America.

Stephen and Willis had just paid a visit to the Bruce family castle, near Staunton, Virginia, about two and a half hours from D.C.

David and Evangeline Bruce's daughter Alexandra had married about this time—not wisely, as it turned out.

At our dinner both Willis and Stephen were in raptures about the treasures in the castle: books, silver, wine.

(During World War II David Bruce had served just under Colonel "Wild Bill" Donovan, in the OSS. David was known as "Bordeaux Bruce" because he seldom allowed the severity of the struggle to keep him from enjoying his favorite vintages. After his death Evangeline published a war diary he kept, which might better have been left unpublished, since what it mainly reveals is David Bruce's detachment from most things human, among them his three children and World War II.)

Our evening with Willis and Stephen left us with a great longing to see the treasures of the Bruce castle: there was said to be a great Buffon bought from Maggs in the thirties, which alone we would have driven to Staunton to see.

We never saw the great Buffon, which, when it reached the auction rooms, made $55,000.

80

___

FOR A TIME, though, we were hopeful. It became known that David Bruce had given the castle and its contents to his children. Maybe they would want to sell some books.

Hopefulness proved to be not enough. No Bruce walked in offering to sell us books—and yet, over time, and by indirection, we did acquire hundreds of books that had once belonged to David K. E. Bruce.

The terrible backstory to these acquisitions was that the Bruces' daughter Sasha either committed suicide or was murdered on the grounds of the Bruce castle. Her recently acquired husband was Greek—he promptly went home to Greece, from which he could not be extradited.

There are two books about David and Evangeline Bruce, a thoroughly hostile one by Joan Mellen and a less hostile but still critical biography of David Bruce by Nelson D. Lankford. The Bruces instigated an investigation into the death of their daughter, but we have never heard the outcome of it.

For a year or two in the mid-seventies James and I moved into the city and lived on O Street in Georgetown, a few doors from the home of David and Evangeline Bruce. We also happened to live right next door to the then prominent antiques dealer Michael Arpad, whose shop itself was only a few more doors east.

I liked Michael Arpad and considered him one of the craftiest dealers I had ever known. One morning as I was walking past his shop Michael leaned out of his door and beckoned me in.

"I have some books you might want," he said. "I got them from the Mellons."

There were in fact about fifty books, all of them scholarly works on Byzantine coinage. Many of them bore the famous Staunton Hill bookplate of a buxom black woman from slave-trading days. The Staunton Hill bookplate had nothing to do with The Brick House, where Paul Mellon once housed his great library before passing most of it on to Yale.

I didn't bother challenging the provenance of these excellent books on Byzantine money. The Mellons and the Bruces were not quite interchangeable, but they came close. David Bruce's first wife had been Ailsa Mellon; she came to David Bruce (I was once told) with a dowry of $10 millon, without which David Bruce would only have been another impoverished aristocrat.

(Huntington Cairns remarked, as we were lunching that day, that there was a club in Baltimore—his hometown—so exclusive that the only person he knew who was in it was David Bruce, who had been put up for it the day he was born. It was called the River Club. Does the River Club still exist? Did it ever?)

Anyway, Michael Arpad's remark to me that he got the Byzantine books from the Mellons was doubly wrong because the books had clearly been collected by Evangeline Bruce's uncle Harold Bell, a well-known Byzantine scholar whose name was in some of them. Michael Arpad surely knew that the books had come from the Bruces, of one generation or another, though he might not have known of Harold Bell.

One day Michael invited me into his house, which was so packed with treasures that I could scarcely squeeze inside.

We promptly bought the books and lined them up on the floor of our shop. David Bruce, who had never been in our shop, walked in the very next day, with a Frenchwoman who was probably an assistant or a keeper.

Ambassador Bruce went across the street to our little annex—it had been our first little shop—where, as luck would have it, Peter Bogdanovich, my friend and then the hottest director in America, was making a long and, I suspect, bombastic phone call. I could see both men clearly from across the street, the distinguished diplomat who had served in London, Paris, Bonn, and Beijing and the newest hot director, who, at the time, had not the slightest inkling of how rapidly and inexorably Hollywood heat could cool.

The Frenchwoman who had come in with David Bruce, like most customers, preferred to look at the books on the floor first—she displayed what I call the midden instinct, an evolutionary throwback to the time when many desirable foodstuffs were buried in middens.

The Frenchwoman, of course, at once saw the Staunton Hill bookplate and promptly had a modest fit. What were we tradesmen doing with David Bruce's books? David Bruce himself luckily returned and gave the books scarcely a glance. He told the woman that he had sold them to Arpad.

I am not sure Marcia and I knew at the time of the death of Sasha Bruce, but we learned about it soon enough when we were visited by a personable former FBI man named Downey Rice. It was he who had been hired by the Bruces to investigate the death of their daughter. The Greek husband, whatever his culpability, was now out of reach.

We sent Downey Rice to Arpad and he received a terrific blast from Mrs. Arpad, a lady known for her terrific blasts.

And that was that, for a while.

81

ONE DAY NOT long after this Willis Van Devanter showed up in our shop, worrying himself over a first edition of Anne Bradstreet's poems. Mistress Bradstreet had been the first American poetess and was herself the subject of a fine tribute: "Homage to Mistress Bradstreet," by John Berryman.

The copy Willis was worrying over had been consigned to him by, I believe, Joseph Alsop. The problem confronting Willis was that the copy whose sale he had been entrusted with was missing a leaf—and, worse yet, a leaf of text, rather than a blank.

Willis Van Devanter, an old friend, is not a man to decide such questions in a flash. Willis never rushed to hasty conclusions. He might weigh the matter for several years before making up his mind.

While Willis was hovering near the door, on the horns of his dilemma, he mentioned that he had taken a workroom near the National Cathedral and was setting up as a bookseller. He invited us to pay him a visit, and we promptly did, although the matter of the missing leaf of text still hung over Willis like a cloud.

Another cloud, if one might call it that, immediately presented itself when we saw the books on offer, most of which bore the Staunton Hill bookplate. Willis, it turned out, was now working for Michael Arpad, who had brought the books in from the castle, along with, probably, much else.

They were just our kind of books: literature, history, sporting books, high-end belles lettres. None of them were the Buffon or, indeed, greatly valuable, but there were well-chosen books and we bought a good many.

The high end of the books from the castle we didn't get, to no one's surprise. Those—including the Buffon—ended up at Christie's, where they did very well.

82

THERE ARE TWO more chapters to the story of the Bruce library at Staunton Hill. Michael Arpad, owner of the books by then, may have been totally on the up-and-up, but it could be that the visit from Downey Rice made him nervous anyway. He no longer wanted the residue of the lesser books around, so he gave them to a local monastic order of some kind, which sold or consigned quite a few Bruce books to a general secondhand shop on Wisconsin called Yesterday's Books.

As soon as I learned that Bruce books were showing up at Yesterday's Books, I made it a practice to go there once a week, and I always came away with several books with David Bruce's signature in them. Most of them were French history and historical biography.

When that trickle stopped we assumed the story was over, but it wasn't. Michael Arpad died, taking his secrets with him. Willis Van Devanter was still worrying about that missing leaf. We never knew who sold the books to Arpad: his sons, his daughter, his son-in-law, or the ambassador himself.

Then one day we got a call from the Folger Library, bastion of Shakespeare studies. It seems that the library had been given some books, many of them French, that didn't really fit into the Folger's plans.

We were there in a jiffy. There were about 250 books in the gift the Folger didn't want. I opened one and there was the well-known bookplate. We thought then that we were buying the last of the books David Bruce accumulated in his lifetime.

But even that was not the end. His sporting books were still to come, including a long run of Derrydale Press books—Derrydale being a publisher that concentrated on fishing, yachting, hunting, quail, dogs, horses, and the like. Some of the Derrydale books were dogs but twenty percent or so were excellent. These books were still in the Bruces' Georgetown house: they were too many and too heavy for John Saumarez Smith to take to Mayfair. We were the next in line.

We paid a hefty price for the sporting books, to Evangeline Bruce, and they were the very last books that we purchased from the Bruce library.

Evangeline Bruce could not have cared less that we were in trade. She happily took our check, and banked it.

I find that I miss her. She has had no real successors. She had been going to teach me about couture, but went blind and never got around to it.

83

In December 1991, I had quadruple bypass surgery at Johns Hopkins Hospital in Baltimore. The trauma this occasioned has been fully described in *Walter Benjamin at the Dairy Queen.* This operation took me out of active book selling for nearly five years, a long and painful interruption.

Fortunately we had at the time a solid stock of some seventy-five thousand volumes in D. C., spread through two buildings and many rooms.

All Marcia had to do was sell them, which she did. But five years is a while; the shelves began to thin out, and while they were thinning out my old friends Lou and Ben Weinstein at the Heritage Book Shop in Los Angeles were having the opposite problem. They needed to make some space and proposed to sell us about five thousand books from the room that held their low-end moderns. Low-end to the Heritage at that juncture was any book priced $500 and down.

That suited us fine. I asked the Weinsteins to do me the favor of sending me Polaroids so we could get a feel for the books, and they did. We studied the Polaroids for a few days and made the deal. The books were sent to D. C. and our stock was nicely perked up.

I returned to full-scale book selling in the mid-nineties, and we continued to buy excellent books. Evelyn Nef, widow of the great Arctic explorer Vilhjamur Stefansson, sold us some. The explorer's main library is at Dartmouth but Evelyn Nef kept some excellent duplicates and was glad to sell them to us.

Thus we acquired the only copy we've ever had of the first grammar of Inuit.

By the mid-nineties, though, it was clear that time had run out for us in Georgetown. The building we occupied would soon be acquired by something more upscale: a Pottery Barn, as it turned out, plus a fancy spa.

Marcia didn't want to give up so we moved back across Thirty-first Street, not far from where we started, and she hung on there for four more years.

We bought Dr. Winifred Whitman's wonderful library, but there were now fifty dealers reasonably nearby, and we ourselves got offered less and less.

In the nineties we began to open satellite stores in a number of cities—mostly for the buying rather than the selling. My old friend Bill Gilliland ran our Dallas store for a while, where we bought an exceptional W. H. Hudson collection and also some excellent books from Lawrence Marcus, including a very respectable Lafcadio Hearn collection.

After a couple of years we sucked Dallas dry and moved on to Houston, where we at once purchased forty-four incunables. In our thirty years of dealing we had owned only one incunable (fifteenth-century book), and that was incomplete, so we were very happy about this coup.

About this time it occurred to me to think about Archer City, mainly because there were a number of cheap, empty buildings there. We shelved one of them and my sister Sue Deen opened and ran a little store called The Blue Pig Bookstore, after the famous pigs in *Lonesome Dove*. The shop was in an old Ford agency, with a knotty-pine showroom and a vast garage, which we first rented to a coffin company. Soon it filled with coffins, but not for long.

My childhood dream of bringing books to Archer City was at last being realized. The citizenry didn't know it yet, but Archer City was on its way to becoming a book town.

84

IN THE 1960s a young English bookseller named Richard Booth began to see possibilities in a modest Welsh village called Hay-on-Wye, now usually shortened to Hay. He began to buy buildings and fill them with books, creating what he considers to be the first real book town. (There are other contenders, of course.)

In Archer City, Booked Up followed suit. We bought building after building and filled them with books. The Blue Pig merged back into Booked Up. Now we own six buildings around the square and five of them are filled with books. Archer City now has a second book business, Three Dog Books.* It also has four banks, which seems a lot of banks.

Richard Booth issues a semiofficial guide to these book towns, and sometimes he visits them and christens them. He had been meaning to come to Archer City, but so far, the weather reports have kept him away.

---

* It recently acquired a third bookman in the person of the scout Mike Stevens.

85

LONG AGO, WHEN I was poking around Joe Petty's bookshop, in Houston, I bought one book that was not by Romain Rolland. It was instead by Arnold Bennett, and its title was *Literary Taste: How to Form It.*

I bought the book and read it several times—if there was anything I lacked just then, it was literary taste.

I didn't know it at the time, but many literary men of Bennett's era were eager to instruct the public in what constituted good taste in literature. When we bought what remained of the stock of the Battery Park bookshop in New York—a shop that specialized in books about books—we acquired sixteen copies of the Arnold Bennett book, and perhaps as many as sixty copies of Andrew Lang's *The Library,* a book issued with the same intent: to show middle-class readers what was correct in literature and what was not.

Both books insisted that a very respectable library could be had for a pittance. Many inexpensive reprint series sprung up, of which the Everyman's series was the best known. In America there would soon be the Modern Library. A few of the early titles in these series became valuable. A little green book in the University series called *Landmarks in French Literature* by one Giles Lytton Strachey was one such, since its author went on to write *Eminent Victorians.*

In the age of the iPod these solemn lectures on what constitutes good literature seem distinctly quaint. Now and then a critic will still cough up a list. Cyril Connolly issued *The Modern Movement,* probably because he owned nice copies of most of the books listed. (Those copies are now in Tulsa, Oklahoma.)

At the turn of the millennium there was a flurry of such lists, none of which made the slightest difference, either to writers or readers.

I know one bookman, who once had at least the semblance of a library, who informed me recently that he already had sixteen hundred songs on his iPod. He didn't mention having bought any books along the way.

It's hard to buck an emerging culture, but pluralism is still possible— one need not really abandon the rich book culture that was there before.

86

By the time Internet book selling became first possible, then actual, Marcia and I thought the matter over and decided we did not want to put our stock online. We were in-shop, off-the-shelf booksellers and that was that. We don't even like to catalogue: in thirty-five years we've issued two. We put attractive books on the shelves and hope that someone will recognize this and walk in, peruse, and purchase.

Our decision was made easier because we are both technology-challenged. I still write on a typewriter and now have some difficulty changing the ribbons. Marcia writes all invoices in longhand. Our able shop manager in Archer City, Khristal Collins, has begun to put books online, and as she persists our online offerings will grow.

At the bottom of our resistance to Internet book selling is our history. We always wanted not just books but a *shop*. Many of our customers have become friends. Like us they enjoy seeing and touching the books. Our stock represents our taste. What fun is there in clicking, compared to the pleasure of handling a fine copy of a rare book?

We understand that we're privileged, but so are many booksellers, so if we're going to do this at all, we might as well do it our way.

87

THE DOWNTURN IN the general antiquarian book selling occurred in our shop in April of 2001. The bursting of the dot-com bubble deprived us at once of two staples of our business: dealers and snow birds. Retired couples from the frigid upper Midwest whose habit had been to winter on the Texas Gulf Coast found they could not afford to spend a month or two on the beaches.

The funny money, to use Mark Singer's phrase, had vanished.

And dealers stopped coming too. Why spend money on overpriced gasoline when they could purchase all they could afford to buy on the Internet?

We did what we always do during sales slumps: we bought. This was not the first slump we had experienced, after all, and our confidence in our stock was strong.

Curiously, in my opinion, the slump that was causing booksellers who sold low- or middling-priced books to close their doors and go home—in most cases the Internet was too slow a tool to save them—had not affected the highest of the high-end dealers and auction houses at all. Book sales at Sotheby's and Christie's were producing record prices, sale after sale. The modern-first market was no exception but it was notable that it had become mostly an inscription market. It was the best moderns with the best inscriptions that produced the record prices.

The sale of Robert Rechler's books, at Christie's in 2003, was a case in point. Here was Faulkner's first book, inscribed to his parents; and Dylan Thomas's first book, likewise inscribed to his parents. There were Graham Greene's novels inscribed to his wife, and Evelyn Waugh's novels inscribed to Graham Greene.

There seemed, suddenly, to be no top. *The New York Times* reports, as I mentioned, that there are now 946 billionaires in America.

When any of these billionaires enters the market for rare books, it is little wonder that there is no ceiling. Not long ago a dealer put $500,000 on a copy of *Prufrock* inscribed by Eliot to the great French poet Paul Valéry. It had been in the Rechler sale, and here it was again, already notched up.

Whether the dealer sold it I don't know. If he did—or if he didn't—it is a copy that is sure to come into the auction rooms again. Those 946 billionaires have to have something to buy.

88

I'VE MENTIONED EARLIER that Booked Up has handled only two great books, the Newton and the Goya.

Then, just as things were winding down in Georgetown, Marcia achieved—with a little help from John Saumarez Smith—a kind of milestone. She sold a book that was worth $100,000.

The book was Winston Churchill's *Marlborough,* the chunky limited edition in 155 copies—not in my mind as attractive a book as the trade edition; but it *was* limited. What made this set a great winner was that it was inscribed in all four volumes to the monarch who was briefly Edward VIII until he abdicated to marry Wallis Simpson: the woman with the molars, as she had sometimes been unkindly described.

Thus the four volumes were inscribed to the Prince of Wales, the Prince of Wales, the king of England, and the duke of Windsor: the same man under three of his titles. The customer who bought the Churchill came from England to take it home.

I believe there is a second such set, similarly inscribed, in the Royal Library, and I believe there was a third set in the house the Windsors lived in in Paris, which now belongs to Mohamed Al Fayed, whose hopes died in a tunnel in Paris in 1997, when his son Dodi was killed in a car wreck, along with Diana, Princess of Wales, and the driver, Henri Paul.

89

IN THE CYBER revolution that we're now in the midst of, where do readers stand?

I am not fully convinced that the big chain stores, Borders and Barnes & Noble, draw off that many readers from the secondhand shops, and if they do, there's a rapid flow-through factor. Since, as nearly as I can tell, few young people are forming personal libraries today, the books bought new at the chains soon trickle back into the secondhand market. Unfortunately there are fewer and fewer secondhand book shops to absorb these shiny new castoffs.

We ourselves are singularly well placed to observe this, since we have now purchased all or part of almost thirty bookshops. It may be that the secondhand book shop will disappear for a while: it almost has, already. In Clegg's dictionary of the world book trade, 1950 edition, there were 175 bookshops in New York City, and that didn't even count the boroughs outside Manhattan. I've mentioned this figure earlier, but it can't hurt to mention it again.

What does any of this say about the most important factor of all, when it comes to books: reading? Book selling will never quite expire unless reading expires first. The secondhand book business, both as a trade and as a subculture, has existed for centuries because people want to read, and the assumption book dealers work on is that people will always want to read.

But will they? Seeing the changes that have occurred in the last few years, I sometimes wonder.

Civilization can probably adjust to the loss of the secondhand book trade, though I don't think it's really likely to have to.

Can it, though, survive the loss of reading?

That's a tougher question, but a very important one.

90

THERE HAVE, IN fact, always been book dealers who prefer to deal from their homes, as Internet book dealers mostly do now. Whether they're dealing by computer and e-mail or with a typewriter and a stack of post-cards may not matter much. The late Richard Mohr of International Bookfinders in Pacific Palisades was one such dealer, and there were many like him.

There was once even a magazine called *Antiquarian Bookman,* which, besides conveying general book trade news, ran the want lists of hundreds of dealers.

Only a dozen years ago, while forming a library for a collector in California, we ran long ads in the *AB* and bought more than four thousand books off the quotations we received.

Like many other Luddites, I regret the loss of the *AB,* as it was called. It was a real book business magazine, rendering an important service. In England there was a similar magazine, called *The Clique,* which did exactly the same thing. *The Clique,* once a year or so, would even publish an odd-volumes issue, to help dealers fill out incomplete sets, providing a very useful service indeed.

91

A CHAPTER OR two back I brought up the matter of reading. What if it does stop? Even now the very successful rise of the audiobook suggests that nearly as many people are being read to as actually read. I don't like the audiobooks but at least they preserve the human longing for narrative, and for a certain linkage between the author and the reader. A story gets told, and loyalties to authors might be developed.

The complex truth is that many activities last for centuries, and then simply (or unsimply) stop. We rarely bleed people now, although it was a common therapy for centuries. (Now, in some quarters, leeches are coming back, which is a hopeful sign.)

In commerce extinctions happen often. It didn't take electricity long to kill off the kerosene lantern.

92

TODAY THE SIGHT that discourages book people most is to walk into a public library and see computers where books used to be. In many cases not even the librarians want books to be there. What consumers want now is information, and information increasingly comes from computers.

That is a preference I can't grasp, much less share, though I'm well aware that computers have many valid uses. They save lives, and they make research in most cases a thing that's almost instantaneous.

They do many good things.

But they don't really do what books do, and why should they usurp the chief function of a public library, which is to provide readers access to books? Books can accommodate the proximity of computers but it doesn't seem to work the other way around. Computers now literally drive out books from the place that should, by definition, be books' own home: the library.

93

VERY QUICKLY, ONCE I had my nineteen books, I realized that reading was probably the cheapest and most stable pleasure of life. Sometimes books excite me, sometimes they sustain me, but rarely do they disappoint me—as *books,* that is, if not necessarily the poetry, history, or fiction that they contain.

I recently fell into a depression that lasted about a year and a half. During that depression my reading habits changed. I had come to admire the diaries of the minor English literary figure James Lees-Milne, author of several not particularly good books on architecture, a few bad novels, a delightful memoir (*Another Self*), several readable biographies, and twelve glorious volumes of the diaries. These diaries (twelve volumes, various publishers, 1975–2005), covering the years 1942 to 1997, do not depend on fact for their appeal: they depend on the charm of the writer's reports both on his own moods and on those of people he was close to. He led a full life, balanced, like most lives, between happiness and frustration. I wrote a small piece about him for *The New York Review of Books;* the issue it appeared in, I'm told, was immediately stolen from all the men's clubs of London, a compliment James Lees-Milne would surely have enjoyed.

As I sank deeper and deeper in depression, I became more and more dependent on the diaries—in time I found that I could read almost nothing else.

I have read the whole twelve volumes several times and I am sure I will keep rereading them for the rest of my life.

The motives for rereading are different from those of first readings, but the rereads are no less valuable for that.

There's no reason, of course, that one can't do both.

94

To the extent that I'm known to the general public at all, I'm known as a novelist whose books make excellent movies—*Hud, The Last Picture Show, Terms of Endearment, Lonesome Dove*—and as the author, along with my partner Diana Ossana, of the Oscar-winning adaptation of Annie Proulx's *Brokeback Mountain*.

Yet, so far in this hasty account of my life with books, I've said almost nothing about my writing. I did mention that, from the first, I banked on regularity. I wrote five pages a day for many years; then, as my fluency increased, I upped the pace to ten pages a day.

At the beginning of my career I very intensely wanted to be a writer, and nothing else. Very quickly I came to realize that I couldn't write anything short. I was neither a poet nor a short story writer. The one short story I ever published in a real magazine (*Texas Quarterly*), called "There Will Be Peace in Korea"—the title was a direct steal from the gospel singer Sister Rosetta Tharpe—was just *The Last Picture Show* in embryo. I was a novelist or I was nothing.

As I went on through life I wrote novel after novel, to the number of about thirty. Most were good, three or four were indifferent to bad, and two or three were really good. None, to my regret, were great, although my long Western *Lonesome Dove* was very popular—the miniseries made from it was even more popular.

Popularity, of course, is not the same as greatness.

225

Greatness, obviously, is rare, a fact I was reminded of recently when I was looking through a wall of books in the Library of America, Edmund Wilson's brainchild and our answer to the Pléiade, the long-established, permanently-in-print editions of French classics.

The Library of America mounts a very respectable effort to make our own classics permanently available in a handy, readable format. I respect it but I don't love it, and every now and then, as the mass of the Library of America grows, doubts arise. At least half of the American books they republish seem to me wholly unreadable, with a few being merely second-rate. The more of our minor fiction they publish, the more they weaken the national brew. The masterpieces tower, as masterpieces should, but beneath them is a lot of literary shrubbery to be pushed through.

This is not likely to be a popular view, but the cruel fact is that many writers go on writing after it would have been better for them to stop. Of course, it's not human nature to stop when you're winning—or even when you just think you're winning, which is more often the case. Among the many inconsistencies that plague writers one is likely to be an inconsistent attitude toward one's own work.

I went for about nine years, from the time I finished *Terms of Endearment* to the time when I began *The Desert Rose,* without writing a single sentence or paragraph that didn't feel as if I'd written that sentence or that paragraph at some point before. In those nine years I eked out only two books, *Somebody's Darling* and *Cadillac Jack,* and didn't like either of them.

Then, through a kind of miracle, I came back. I was sent to Las Vegas to write about the real life of a showgirl, and instead wrote the short, but to me appealing, *Desert Rose.*

The character Harmony, the showgirl being replaced in her own show by her own daughter, lifted my spirits to such a degree that I began to feel like a novelist again. I went on to write about twenty more novels, including another, darker book about Harmony, called *The Late Child.*

95

DURING THE NINE dark years when I didn't like my own writing, a tension developed between writing and reading that has not abated to this day, and this despite the fact that the two activities ought to be complementary. But are they? When I'm writing I often spin out my daily pages as rapidly as possible, in order to get back to whatever I am reading.

It may be that a little frisson between writing and reading is not a bad thing. Mostly the reading fertilizes the writing, and this is a constant process. Reading is the aquifer that drips, spongelike, into my fiction. (I owe the figure to Robert B. Parker, in *Potshot*.)

It also drips slowly into my nonfiction, of which there are now eleven books.

96

THE SECOND AND more powerful competitor to writing is, of course, book selling, or perhaps I should say book buying, because the buying end of the trade always interests me more than the selling end.

Since our store was on a major street in Georgetown, we were well positioned from the first to sell with a minimum of effort. If we found appealing books in the right condition, the selling, for a long time, took care of itself.

By this time, of course, I had been writing on a daily basis for thirty years, and screenwriting for nearly that long. Writing was by then neither a keen pleasure nor a hated chore. It was simply my vocation.

What always bothered me most about writing was that it was sedentary. I was born to working-class people. Getting up and then sitting down to peck at a strange machine didn't seem like work compared to what my father did.

Book hunting, shelving, arranging, pricing was *active*. It was physically taxing, if we were moving a library—but it always retained an intellectual dimension.

Eventually book selling took more and more of my energies. I still tried to write scrupulously, but a point was reached after which I was probably more interested in finding the right book than I was in seeking the mot juste.

Flaubert, for that matter, could not always locate the mot juste either. Try *Salammbô* or *La Tentation de Saint Antoine* sometime.

Hard work there needs to be, but fanaticism? Joyce and Stein and one or two others are dead ends and were meant to be dead ends for the writers who followed them. Who is going to go on from *Finnegans Wake* or *The Making of Americans*?

97

THE ANTIQUARIAN BOOK trade is an anecdotal culture. In any era one or two booksellers will usually manage to be, for a time, the focus of the trade's attention. The famous Dr. A. S. W. Rosenbach was one such, but he operated at the high end, whereas most booksellers, like it or not, are low-end. Many of the best are both poor and odd. The small Jewish man in San Francisco who operated his high-shelved shop behind the *San Francisco Chronicle* where customers used binoculars, was both poor and odd. Not lunatic odd, perhaps, but bookseller odd.

The writer who should have written a masterwork about the second-hand book trade was Anton Chekhov, the genius of small frustrations and little failures. Chekhov had a natural sympathy for fringe cultures.

When I began scouting, the secondhand book trade was not yet a fringe culture. Of course, there were plenty of fringe people in the book trade, but bookshops were still accepted, in the way that barbershops and hardware stores were accepted.

Fifty years have made a big difference. The people of my hometown seem to be a little uncomfortable with our three hundred thousand books, although the stock is passive and has attacked no one.

How did one of the pillars of civilization come, in only fifty years, to be mostly unwanted?

I have no satisfactory answer to that, but I do have a few anecdotes.

One day I was sitting alone behind our desk about noon when a six-foot-two black transvestite in a yellow miniskirt came walking in, drinking a Coke from a bottle. He/she seemed exuberant, rather than menacing, though that soon changed.

"Do you have any books by Mark Twain?" he/she asked.

Unfortunately we didn't—we usually do have a good selection of Mark Twain, but that day, we were fresh out.

"Then I should just kill you, shouldn't I?" he/she asked, when I confessed our lack of Twain.

"Gosh," I said.

Since this particular lady/gentleman was often to be seen around Georgetown, I didn't feel myself to be in much danger.

Just then my customer spotted a rival across the street and went rushing out the door and threw her Coke bottle at the rival, missing, but not by much.

One day a woman in her thirties, quite good looking, pulled up to our curb in a rattly car and she too, once she was in, asked if we had any Mark Twain.

This time we were ready. We had a very nice copy of *Life on the Mississippi,* as well as several attractive editions of his many books.

The lady put the Twain on the desk, which suggested to us that she meant to buy it. It was almost the lunch hour. The lady even mentioned that she was on her way to lunch. But glancing around, she noticed that there were lots more books on the shelves, most of them not by Mark Twain.

Slowly, almost dreamily, she began to work her way around the bookshelves, taking down a book here and there. Marcia showed up and began to invoice the books. The total kept rising until it was close to $10,000, not the kind of sale we were accustomed to making on an otherwise slow day.

The lady took stock of herself and looked at her watch. Then she asked if she could use the phone.

232

"I think I need to call my banker and see if he'll make me a small loan," she said.

The banker was agreeable; we loaded the books into the rattly car; the lady wrote a check and drove blithely off to her lunch.

We could scarcely believe our good fortune.

Five years later the same lady drove up in a different car—this one didn't rattle—and sold us every last one of the books back. A few of them had surged in price—we were delighted to be able to sell them again.

Most booksellers, of course, delight in getting their treasures back, so they can sell them again. Peter Howard of Serendipity Books has twice sold the great copy of *The Sound and the Fury* with the "I put my living guts into this" inscription.

Peter got the book in the first place from Max Hunley, the crafty dealer whom I've already mentioned, who loved to outlive his customers, get his books back, and sell them again. The last time I saw Max he showed me a true first of *Daisy Miller,* which he was preparing to sell for the third time.

Speaking of the practice of reselling rare books, not for nothing did Lou and Ben Weinstein, of the Heritage Book Shop, choose the movie capital in which to set up their stall. There are few towns more fickle, and certainly few with fresher money, than L.A. I was with Peter Bogdanovich one day when the Heritage called and offered him a complete set of the books published by the Limited Editions Club, a fancied-up line of reprints of which about ten have any intrinsic worth.

Peter Bogdanovich was not even a book collector, but Lou and Ben are nothing if not salesmen. In a matter of hours the Limited Editions Club, in all its expensive vulgarity, adorned the Bogdanovich shelves, where they were accompanied, eventually, by a nice first of *Walden* and a Second (or was it a Third?) Folio.

All the books soon returned to the great building on Melrose Avenue, where so many upward-moving talents were happy to buy certified classics in the right conditon to give as presents to the director they had just finished wrapping a film with. The present should cost about $40,000 and the brothers Weinstein will be sure to have one waiting.

Or they once would have. Now the Heritage Book Shop is no more.

98

Over the years Marcia and I did a certain amount of appraising. Sometimes it was just work, but sometimes it had interesting results.

One day we were out in northwest Washington, appraising a library that had a lot of good ballooning books in it.

At some point I picked up a hefty book called *The Whale,* our old friend *Moby-Dick* under its English title. *The Whale* is usually found in three volumes, published by the venerable firm of Bentley.

The fat creature I held in my hand was the whole *Whale,* but it appeared from a note in the book that this copy had been the working copy of the once acclaimed, now forgotten author Charles Reade, famous for *The Cloister and the Hearth,* whose job was to edit *The Whale* down to a handier and possibly more salable one-volume edition.

We were unable to buy this book, but we did note that Charles Reade was not a man to be intimidated by a mere American classic.

He began his editorial work by drawing a bold line through "Call me Ishmael."

99

NINETEEN SIXTY-TWO WAS a pivotal year for me—it saw the birth of my son, James. He came along on March 18 and the question I had to answer pretty soon was how to pay for his arrival. I was teaching five classes at TCU, but salaries for young instructors were at that time modest. Babies didn't fit into the budget, and the movie money for *Hud* had yet to arrive.

I owned at this time about four hundred books. I didn't think of them as a collection, or of myself as a collector. I was merely a beginning novelist. The Beat Generation was happening and all, but mainly what I did was grade papers.

It soon became apparent that if I wanted to pay this modest hospital bill, I would need to sell books.

My friends Bill and Anne Gilliland were nice enough to let me hold a book sale in their living room in Dallas. There I parted with my fine copy of *Go,* the novel by John Clellon Holmes that preceded *On the Road* in the chronology of Beatdom. Two or three other novels arguably preceded it, but Kerouac's book was so much better than any of the others that it became, and remains, the keynote of Beat fiction. (The scroll version, in my opinion, is better still.)

As luck would have it a man named Harry Sivia, later a friend, showed up at this sale and bought the whole schmear. It turned out that Harry was looking to go into the secondhand book business, and he did go into it, operating for several years as the Texas Bookman, from various locations around Dallas.

In those feckless days Jo and I often wrote our names in the books we bought, and sometimes we wrote them in ink. When we bought them we never supposed we'd be selling them, or that the presence of our names would make the slightest difference to the buyer. Thousands of innocents write their names in books. Why not?

Why not is because, in the collector's market, having someone's name in the book is a blemish—unless, of course, the person whose name it was was famous, as I then was not.

Harry Sivia, now "late" as the Botswanians say, shared some traits with Joe Btfsplk, the unlucky character in *L'il Abner* who goes around with a personal raincloud over his head. Joe Btfsplk just couldn't win, and neither could Harry Sivia. Harry spent a long time sanding my name out of those books, and just about the time he finished, my name had begun to add to, rather than subtract from, the value of the book.

I have now reacquired about sixty books that I owned during this period. Most of them were bought in the Dallas area and probably represent books Harry hadn't got around to with his sander.

The silent migration of books is fascinating to me. I know a collector in Virginia who claims he lost one volume of Douglas Carruthers's two-volume *Unknown Mongolia* while traveling in the Gobi Desert, only to reacquire the lost volume several years later in Estate Book Sales in Washington, D.C.

100

AT ONE TIME in my early years as a book scout I often dreamt of books I might find the next day while scouting. Indeed, over the last half century, I've averaged five or six dreams a year about book buying. Usually, in these dreams, I'm hurriedly scouting a bookshop I've never been in before—or else I'm alone in a large library. The books I'm looking at are quite vivid to me—they look very much like books I've handled before, or seen in auction catalogues; and yet they are never an exact match. I'm dreaming about books that are very much like other books I've handled, and yet they aren't the exact books that are on my shelves. They seem to be books I'm going to find soon. I think of them as dream children, of the sort Charles Lamb wrote about.

1O1

I'VE CHOSEN, FOR the most part, to keep this memoir personality-free. Attempting to interest twenty-first-century readers in the personalities of (mainly) twentieth-century bookmen risks making this narrative more circumscribed than I want it to be. Who among today's readers needs to know about booksellers who are, in the Botswanian term, "late"?

Should Warren Howell have bought that last suspect bunch of books? Did Johnny Jenkins gamble unwisely? Was H. P. Kraus ever friendly? And so on. We should, as Rilke cautions, let the dead be dead: they have their sphere and we have ours.

Years ago I had a famous quarrel with the book-selling fraternity over the trade in film scripts, a practice so universal now that it's pointless even to discuss it. But I've earned most of the money I've used to build Booked Up by working on film scripts—nearly seventy of them in at least one draft—so I come at the problem from a very different angle.

The matter of vanishing bookshops is far more urgent. I can't keep them from vanishing, but in many cases I can welcome a lot of their stock into our stock, even at the risk of substantial duplication. We currently have over one hundred copies of one Nicholson Baker book, and almost as many of a play by Cormac McCarthy, though the latter have recently begun to slip away.

102

LIFE IN THE world of goods—as the great anthropologist Mary Douglas calls it—seems to be natural to me. I like buying better than I like selling, but I can do either and not lose sleep.

It's clear from what I said about Janet Auchincloss that pockets of the monied still exist; there are people who just don't know how to sell things, although sometimes they are able to learn. I knew a gentleman who grew up in a household that held two Audubon *Birds of America* in the double elephant folio edition, worth millions now.

For a long time, I suspect, the lucky owner of two Audubons never suspected that fell chance would bring him to consider that a family possession might be salable and might even be sold.

In time, though, many gentlefolk from here and the British Isles have learned to sell and have become quite good at it. I don't know where the Audubons went, but when I knew the man he still had one priceless possession and, besides, something not priceless but very desirable: a wooden eighteenth-century brothel sign. It was as good a thing as a narwhal tusk, but like the narwhal tusk, we didn't get it.

I have known successful booksellers who master the art of selling but neglect the equally important art of buying. Even those who do know how to buy often find themselves so hard-pressed by the extraordinary rise in the price of modern rarities that they have to form partnerships in order to compete. (In comic book dealing the most expensive issues have long since been owned mainly by syndicates.)

This is more and more the case in the ownership of the really expensive rare books.

103

EARLY IN 2005 I made what will probably be my last adventure in mass book buying. Fifty-five thousand books were involved; they filled a large house and no less than twenty-seven Tuff Sheds in Pasadena, California.

The Mesa Book Company, which we had purchased earlier, had almost that many books, but in that case the owners packed them. All I had to do was go home and help unpack them.

I was a few years younger then, and I still assumed that I could, if need be, pack any amount of books, and move them. I was rounding on seventy, but so what?

Now I know what!

The books in Pasadena had belonged to a well-read woman named Edith Waldron. Just the other day I was unpacking some books from Berkeley and there was a book with Edith Waldron's attractive bookplate in it—a bookplate I had never seen before—and seeing it gave me an eerie feeling. That book had come winging in from Berkeley to join thousands of its mates.

Some months earlier I received a call about the Waldron books from Basil Jenkins, the gentleman who had been entrusted with the task of selling them. At first I thought he must be kidding. Fifty-five thousand books? And us still modestly funded! I assumed we had no chance. Many dealers far better heeled than we were would no doubt hurry to snatch up this prize.

Still, no bookman whose heart was still beating would turn down a chance to bid—so out to Pasadena I went. Edith Waldron had, for a time, kept a modest shop in San Marino—I visited it once, on the advice of Max Hunley, but since she specialized in occulta I didn't buy much. I knew she was big in metaphysical circles and may even have played tennis with Krishnamurti, but she was not in the shop that day and I never met her.

Anyway, Basil Jenkins assured me I would find the books interesting, and I did. The minute I saw them I wanted them, and yet I rated my chance of getting them as poor to none. After all, Powell's (Portland, Oregon) had been there, as well as—I assumed—behemoths closer to hand, such as the Book Baron in Anaheim, a shop run by Bob Weinstein, brother of Lou and Ben. (No less than seventeen members of the Weinstein family were at that time in the book business—this is Ben Weinstein's count.) The Book Baron was certainly the dealer of any size closest to the Waldron books.

I looked and I looked, but could not long avoid the moment of truth. I asked Basil how high I would have to go to acquire this prize, and he at once told me that so far there had been no bids.

No bids?

I think it was at that moment that I realized what poor shape the American antiquarian book trade actually was in. Edith Waldron had been a woman of taste. Her library contained a few expensive books, plus many thousands that were attractive without being very particularly expensive. One Tuff Shed turned out to contain nothing but books by the Reverend Sabine Baring-Gould. How often does a shed full of Baring-Gould's three-deckers fall in your lap? Who could turn that down?

Everyone but me turned it down. I bought the books for a considerable if modest sum and was and remain very happy with my purchase.

104

It was not until I returned to Pasadena that the daunting aspects of the deal came clear to me. I had fifty-five thousand books and no packing staff, no trucks, no nothing.

After a day or two of solitary packing I called in our old friends Bill Hale and Candee Harris, and I also recruited a local friend named Janice. Soon a team was assembled and went to work.

From the first I knew that I would have to divide the Waldron books, so I called Robert Schlesinger of Bookman's, in Tucson. Bookman's is a small chain looking to expand, and they had the muscle we lacked and easily found the trucks. We kept about ten thousand books for ourselves.

I sealed the deal by buying Robert and his colleague Scott an excellent vegetarian burrito at a small carryout nearby.

An irony lost on everyone but myself was that just next door to the Mexican carryout was a much more iconic carryout: the original In-N-Out Burger. Eating there was a little like eating at the first McDonald's— only better.

105

As a dealer who has accumulated hundreds of thousands of books, one practice I consider essential is the purge. My job, when I'm at my pricing table in Booked Up, is to be a junk rejecter. The bane of large secondhand book dealers is that junk inevitably seeps in, and the iron rule is that good books do not pull bad books up: bad books pull good books down. A shop whose shelves are not regularly purged of junk will soon look like a junk shop.

Once a purge—which could now involve several thousand volumes—is completed, we're always surprised at how much better the stock looks.

In a normal year we will take in about two thousand boxes. One of my chief pleasures is to unpack and sort these books—the junk we downstream, to flea-marketers, nearby libraries, or anyone we can find who will take them. The fact that the shelves of Booked Up are almost entirely junk free is perhaps our main distinction.

106

WHEN WE BOUGHT the low-end moderns from the Heritage Book Shop in the early nineties, we didn't realize that a new book-buying methodology was being created. Since then we've bought more than a dozen libraries or book stocks just by persuading the owners to pick up a Polaroid or a camcorder and make us some pictures of what is being sold.

In fact, having the captured image enables us to examine the books more closely than we would if we were in the shop with them.

We now do this routinely—it saves a lot of travel time. Perhaps my happiest experience with camcorder buying involved a bookshop in Lincoln, Nebraska, that we had been offered. I didn't have time to go trucking up the road to Lincoln, so the owner very nicely made us a video. Most of his books were duplicates, but as I was peering at these faraway shelves from the comfort of my couch I noticed a greenish book nestled in with some boys' books—boys' books not very different from the nineteen Robert Hilburn had sent me so long ago.

I looked at the greenish book several times and determined that it was definitely not a boy's book. Instead, it was a legendary *New Yorker* book: Joseph Mitchell's *My Ears Are Bent:* his early journalism, most of it pre–*New Yorker.* It cost me $18, $3 of which was postage.

107

ONE DAY A nice young man came walking into our bookshop and looked around with something like awe.

"My mom's boss would probably buy this whole bookshop, if he could see it," he said.

We demurred, though we liked the young man, who returned a few days later and repeated his remark.

Two weeks or so along his mom herself called. Her name was Mary Ellen Compliment, and she was calling from Pittsburgh. Mary Ellen hit us with a pretty startling request.

Her boss, she said, had heard that I had a really good library.

I acknowledged that I did indeed have a good library.

What her boss would like, she said, was for us to sell him three copies of every book in my library.

Whoa!

"Why three?" I asked.

"One for him and one for each of his daughters," she replied.

His two daughters were, at the time, both under six.

I mentioned that it had taken me forty years to assemble my library; and, I added, burdening young children with thousands of books was the surest way to make them hate reading, in my opinion.

We liked Mary Ellen Compliment, though, and we did at least manage to find out the name of the man who had made the extraordinary request.

His name was Joe Pytka, of Pittsburgh, Malibu, New York, Paris, and Santa Fe.

In Hollywood, Joe Pytka (director of two movies and many, many award-winning commercials) is a living legend, mainly because he has hired and fired and rehired and refired half the crew people in Hollywood. He happens also to be a restaurateur who bought the largest truffle of the year at the French truffle auction a few years back. He has either houses or apartments in all the aforenamed places, and none of them, apparently, contained enough books.

108

INTO OUR LIVES, about this time, came a personality about as distant from Joe Pytka's as it would be possible to go: Robert Manson Myers, famous mainly for two books, the satire *From Beowulf to Virginia Woolf* and the huge collection of Civil War letters called *The Children of Pride,* which he edited and, in time, began to give readings from.

Manson, as we came to know him, is a consummate Georgian figure. He was about to retire from a distinguished teaching career, with a concentration on the eighteenth century. He had a wonderful library: all the necessary eighteenth-century texts, and the scholarship that accompanied them. He also kept, for bedside reading, good collections of many lady novelists: Ivy Compton-Burnett, Elizabeth Bowen, Elizabeth Spencer, and many more.

He also had, shelved in a special nook of his perfect Georgian drawing room, 999 of the first thousand volumes of Everyman's Library: all the early, flat-spined Everyman's, in wonderful condition. Manson was always very picky about condition. We bought many of his books, including the Everyman's collection.

Meanwhile Joe Pytka still wanted us to sell him lots of books. Mary Ellen Compliment had mentioned that he had a Paris apartment. Robert Manson Myers was about to move to London, where he had another splendid Georgian apartment.

How nice, it seemed to us, if his Everyman's collection could come to rest in Paris, more or less nearby.

This happy solution immediately came to pass. We mentioned a figure to Mary Ellen Compliment, and a check from Pittsburgh arrived the next day.

Meanwhile, to see that Joe Pytka had books other than in Paris, we made a careful list of all the books in the humanistic fields that a book lover and man of parts should have.

I made the list, and we began to search for the books on it. Joe accepted every shipment happily.

After three years of this I myself drove a van full of books to Venice, California, where Joe has his offices and studio. I did this mainly because I wanted to meet the man. At the time he was far and away our best customer.

That I was actually hands-on in delivering him books probably horrified Joe—he soon came racing down from Malibu with his beautiful wife, Emmanuelle. When they arrived Joe flung himself at the boxes much as Scrooge McDuck flings himself into his money bin. (In Scandinavia, I understand, Scrooge McDuck is studied in colleges as a model of capitalistic method.)

The last load we sent Joe, to his adobe on the Plaza in Santa Fe, came from the library of Peter Hurd and Henriette Wyeth, who had their studios not far away, in the Hondo Valley.

I don't want to go on telling endless fish stories, but I will say that the fact that Robert Manson Myers's impeccable Everyman's collection now lives in Joe Pytka's Paris apartment convinces me yet again what a wonderful, small-worldish trade book selling is.

109

As workers in an ancient trade we feel, with Whitman, part of all that we have met; and those that we have met in book selling are part of us in the most tangible of ways: their books, though in diminishing numbers (we hope), remain on our shelves.

We feel Booked Up to be a kind of anthology of bookshops past—or, that is, past and ongoing. We list below the dealers from whom we have bought in bulk, or else bought from so steadily over the years that the books that came from them amount to bulk. The list is in no order. There are a few notes.

William F. Hale Books, Washington, D.C. We bought his store stock twice.
Candee Harris, Logic and Literature, D.C. Ditto.
Second Story Books, D.C./Maryland. Thousands.
Joseph the Provider, Santa Barbara, California. Splintered now.
Conrad's Bookshop, Fourth Avenue, Tucson, Arizona. Gone.
Mesa Book Company, Mesa, Arizona. Gone.
Robert Hecht, Paradise Valley, Arizona. We have his natural history.
Einer Nissula, Fountain Valley, Arizona. Stock purchased but he has re-plenished.
A Book Buyer's Shop, Houston, Texas. Run by Chester and Christine Dobie; bought stock twice.
Detering Book Gallery, Houston, Texas.

Micklestreet Books, East Lebanon, Maine. Wright IV fiction.

Serendipity Books, Berkeley, California. Many thousands.

Melvin McCosh, Excelsior, Minnesota. Many thousands.

G. Heywood Hill, 10 Curzon Street, London. Books from the Royal Society of Literature.

Phoenix Bookshop, New York City. Acquired, at one remove, from Second Story.

Paulette Greene First Editions, New York. Ditto.

Michael Ginsburg, Sharon, Massachusetts.

Black Oak Books, Berkeley, California.

Heritage Book Shop, Los Angeles. Gone.

The Book Baron, Anaheim, California.

Canterbury Bookshop, Los Angeles. Gone.

Michael Thompson, Los Angeles. Our wonderful Africana.

Norman and Michal Kane, Pottstown, Pennsylvania. Store stock.

Old Oregon Bookshop, Portland. Espionage books.

Powell's Books, Portland, Oregon.

Quill and Brush, Dickerson, Maryland.

Antiquarian Shop, Scottsdale, Arizona. New ownership; George Chamberlain dead.

William & Nina Matheson Books. Chevy Chase, Maryland.

Carnegie Bookshop, New York City.

Bartleby's Books, D.C.

Riverrun, Dobbs Ferry, New York. Thousands.

Three Dog Books, Archer City, Texas. Neighbors.

Bauman Rare Books, Philadelphia. My skull collection.

Thomas Boss, Boston. The stock of the Battery Park bookshop.

Brick Row Bookshop, San Francisco.

Franklin Gilliam Rare Books, Charlottesville, Virginia.

John Gach Books, Randall's Ferry Town, Maryland. Many hundreds.

Anthony Garnett, St. Louis.

Laurence McGilvery, La Jolla, California.

Park Bookshop, D.C. Gone.

Barber's Book Store, Fort Worth, Texas.

Nicolas Potter, Santa Fe, New Mexico.

Sam Weller's Zion Bookshop, Salt Lake City, Utah.

Lost Generation, St. Louis, Missouri.

Allan Milkerit Books, San Francisco. Gone.

Dutton's, Los Angeles. Gone.